Successful Change Man

Successful Change Management

The fifty key facts

Gwen Ventris

continuum
LONDON • NEW YORK

658.406
VEN

Continuum International Publishing Group

The Tower Building
11 York Road
London SE1 7NX

15 East 26th Street
New York,
NY 10010

© Gwen Ventris 2004

British Library Cataloguing-in-Publication Data

A catalogue record for this book is available from the British Library.

ISBN 0–8264–7205–2 (paperback)

Typeset by YHT Ltd, London
Printed and bound in Great Britain by Antony Rowe Ltd., Chippenham, Wiltshire

Contents

Foreword *by Adam Morgan*   vii
Introduction   1

Part One: The Change Drivers   3

1   What is change management?   5
2   Choosing the right changes   8
3   Changing cultures   10
4   Changing the paradigm   13
5   Change in three dimensions   16
6   The benefit of a major crisis   18
7   The price of avoiding the culture of change   20
8   Preparing for the journey   22

Part Two: Planning and Launching your Change Programme   25

9   The timing of change management   27
10   Creating a crystal-clear vision   30
11   Planning ahead of the change curve   32
12   Being blind to the past   34
13   Bite-size change management   36
14   Changing when things are going well   38
15   Keeping in touch with customer expectations   40
16   Change due to competition   42
17   When whole organizations face change   44
18   Risk analysis and management   46
19   Leading and managing the process   48
20   When to use change management consultants   50
21   Return on investment (money)   52
22   Return on investment (people)   54
23   Effective communication   57
24   The power of accountability   60
25   Presenting the case for change   62
26   Selling the dream   66

Part Three: Leading and Managing Change Successfully 69

27 Making the vision a reality 71
28 Articulating the strategy 73
29 Trusting the new broom 75
30 Changing attitudes to authority 77
31 Putting wrong changes right 79
32 Facing the financial truth 81
33 Combating resistance to change 83
34 The importance of feelings 86
35 Technology take-up 89
36 Changing role-based cultures 91
37 Working with trade unions to bring about change 93
38 When things get personal 95
39 Establishing milestones 97
40 Starting at the top 99
41 Supporting the leader 102
42 Uncovering the current culture 104

Part Four: Profiting from your Success 107

43 Creating a 'joined-up' organization 109
44 Recognition and reward systems 111
45 Recruiting for change 113
46 Changing people's perceptions of themselves 116
47 Training for change 118
48 Changing attitude: the party test 120
49 Measures of success 122
50 Maintaining a permanent evolution 125

Foreword

There is a tendency to think of change management as a kind of occasional 'intervention' – a convulsive act of rebirth with a messianic beginning and a celebrated end, requiring a visionary leader, an unquestioning love of wild-eyed chaos, and perhaps only made a little more accessible by an informal study of the movements of mice and cheese.

And if an enthusiasm for this kind of thinking is what gets you out of bed in the morning, then I'm going to have to ask you to pass right along – for *Successful Change Management* is perhaps the first change management book for the rest of us. It is one of those books that very quietly dismantles one by one many of the intimidating myths that surround this critical area, and rebuilds in their place, brick by measured brick, a way of thinking about managing change in our own organization which is so practical and so well-considered that by the end we cannot imagine why we found 'This whole change thing' so daunting in the first place. Don't be fooled by how easy a book it is to read, or what approachable common-sense each bite-sized lesson seems to be in isolation – the cumulative effect is to increase not just our confidence and understanding but also our appetite to play a personal part in the ongoing evolution of our companies.

For, beneath the step-by-step advice, increasing that appetite in all of us is Gwen Ventris's ultimate ambition. Her view is that change in any organization needs to be constant rather than occasional – requiring of course not just a day-to-day understanding but also a day-to-day desire. In this sense Gwen's book is at once a guide and a spur. For Gwen is not an ivory-tower academic; she is one of the most dynamic practitioners of change I have ever met, and, as a practitioner, what she is interested in is making things happen. Not next year. Not intermittently. But constantly. And here. And now.

These are of course not 50 independent thoughts; they are 50 interconnected steps of the same journey. And, personally, if I was making that journey, there is no one I can think of whom I would rather have forging the way with me than Gwen.

Adam Morgan*

*Author of *Eating the Big Fish: How Challenger Brands Can Compete against Brand Leaders* (Chichester: John Wiley 1999)

Introduction

Companies that stand still, even for a moment, start to die. That's because the demands of customers in every market, from cars and confectionery to banking and battleships, change constantly. And your competitors know this. Successful companies are always striving to stay ahead of their markets as they change. But how do you go about changing a company? More importantly, how do you create a culture of change so an organization can continually address the current needs of its customers?

These are the questions that this book will answer. It will explain why all organizations must practise change management, and practise it well. It will also explain why company leaders and managers need to be the driving forces behind change programmes if they want them to succeed. It will tell you when and why you will meet resistance from your own people, many of whom may fear change. The book will then show you how to start the change process, how to overcome that resistance, bring people on-side and win through. It will take you through the stages listed below of what amounts to a journey, to ensure that you end up at the destination you want to reach and finally create a culture of change in your organization:

1. Helping you to work out what your vision should be; your big idea; the lighthouse message that will navigate your company through the change programme.
2. Guiding you towards creating an overall strategy for achieving that vision and the selection of a change management team to help you deliver it.
3. Keeping you focused on your objective by establishing a plan of action and clear measures of success using a series of achievable milestones.

4. Helping you to focus on developing a communications strategy to support the programme plan.
5. Showing you how to identify and manage risks to the programme: events or factors that might delay or disrupt it.
6. Explaining how you must sell the benefits of the initiative in different ways to various audiences, possibly including some external ones.
7. Assisting you with the task of understanding and dealing with the myriad of complex, personal, emotional and political pressures that confront all managers of change.
8. Planning strategies for dealing with all the challenges you will meet and linking these to the overall implementation plan.
9. Developing a system for maintaining a watch on the market to ensure that the vision for change is always valid and relevant.
10. Determining how you will prove that your programme has been successful and has generated a good return on investment, using a wide range of robust measures. Finally, the book will explain the need to celebrate your success and build on it!

Change management is all about inspirational leadership, detailed planning and rigorous, comprehensive implementation. But first you must know the FACTS ...

Part One:
The Change Drivers

1   What is change management?

'Things must change or cease.'
William Shakespeare

Think of all the major changes in your life. You can probably still remember how you felt on your first day at secondary school or the moment when you finally waved goodbye to your home and family and began life as an independent adult. Then there were all the job changes that meant you had to fit in with new people and work environments and realign your loyalties to different employers and business cultures. Anyone who has had to cope with the sudden death of a close friend or family member may have had their whole outlook on life changed in an instant. Then there are the changes brought about by events such as marriage or divorce, becoming a parent and then a grandparent, retiring or moving house; the list goes on and on. They all have an emotional impact on us in one way or another.

Now ask yourself which of those changes were the most traumatic. The chances are that they were the ones that were not planned or managed in a controlled way. In many cases you knew that these changes were going to happen and when they were going to occur. Indeed, you planned and prepared for them on both a personal and practical level. You knew, for instance, that having children would change your life, so you took certain actions in advance: you probably went out and bought baby clothes, cots, toys and a good stock of nappies. You possibly transformed a bedroom in your house into a nursery. You might even have rethought your finances, taking into account that you or your partner might not have wanted to return to work immediately. All these actions show that you were planning for this big change in your life. You had a vision of how you wanted things to turn out and you took various steps to ensure they happened as planned. That's change management.

When you plan well, the change process should be exciting, rewarding and ultimately successful.

Think of the way you might decide on the outcome of, say, a big house move, perhaps to a new area or even a different country. You start with a positive vision of how you would want your family to feel once the move has been completed. Then you work out all the component parts of delivering that vision – moving house, finding new schools, getting to know a strange environment, and so on. Then you plan how you are going to bring about the changes needed in all those fields. You sell the vision to your family, show them what needs to be done to achieve it and then involve them in the process of making it a reality. You are able to judge your success by the scale of the gap between the vision you portrayed to your family and the experience they will have once the move has been completed.

But what happens when you don't do this, when you try to bring about major change without the vision, the planning and the processes? Never mind happy thoughts about taking life as it comes. It never works. Imagine that major house move without your change management. Think of the family rows, the unhappiness and the disappointment.

Of course major change sometimes occurs suddenly, without warning. Your long-term partner ups and leaves; your company is taken over or goes bust. You cannot plan or prepare yourself for changes like these. And they invariably cause huge distress. Why? It's not just the speed or even the nature of the change that has the most destructive impact. What really makes a difference is the fact that you had no change management process in place: there was no vision and no plan; there were no milestones in the journey from one position to another. In other words, you were not preparing for change and moving towards the delivery of a vision. The change just landed on you out of the blue. And nobody, however adaptive, flexible and open-minded they may consider themselves to be, is able to cope well with change under these circumstances.

Yet that is exactly what we must all learn to do in business today: cope with unexpected change by accepting, as we mentioned earlier, that only through constant change can companies and the people who work for them be successful.

Wouldn't it be great if all companies could have a sort of corporate bath containing magic 'change' fluid? All you would have to do would be to dip all your people in this pool and they would come out ready and willing to accept that change is as much a part of business life as making profits for shareholders. But instead of a dip we have change management. This is the magic fluid that will enable you not just to take your organization through a major change but also at the same time to create the permanent flexible and adaptive culture that you need in order to survive in today's business environment.

Let's go back to the example of the family house move for a moment. If you manage that process effectively, your family's experience will be a positive one. They will accept that change can be good. They could do it again if they had to – no problem.

This is the holy grail of change management in business. Once people have a good change management experience, and recognize the need for almost continuous development in order for their organization to survive and prosper, you will have succeeded in bringing about a culture of continuous change.

But let's be clear about one thing right from the word go: you must eat, sleep and breathe your vision for change. You must believe in the whole idea from top to bottom and have total confidence in your ability to turn it into reality. And you are going to have to keep the flame of change burning in your organization long after your first change management project has been completed.

KEY FACT

An effective change management programme can help you create a culture of continuous change in your organization. But first you must get your people to believe in the value of change.

2 Choosing the right changes

*'Change is inevitable. In a progressive country change is
constant.'*
Benjamin Disraeli

If it's important for you to believe in the need for change yourself,
then it's crucial for everyone else in your organization to do the
same. Never underestimate people's potential for cynicism and
doubt: if they can see the slightest hole in the vision or the plan for
getting there, then they can make life very difficult for the change
manager.

The bottom line is that you must have a genuine reason for
change, one that people in your organization understand and
accept.

Let's look at an example. In the years before British Airways was
privatized (in early 1987), it was clear that the company had to go
through massive change if it were to survive as an independent
airline in a competitive international market which was itself being
restructured at the time. Costs were far too high; working practices
required a complete overhaul; and new technology was needed
throughout the organization. People working in the soon-to-be
privatized airline recognized that wholesale change, indeed a
complete new culture, would be required if the company were to
succeed. They also understood that several change management
exercises would be needed to deliver the vision of 'the world's
favourite airline'.

Like all airlines, BA has had its ups and downs in recent years.
But the key point is that it would not even be in business today if
the people who worked for the company in the 1980s had not
bought the new vision and accepted that their future depended on
its success.

The BA experience illustrates two important points. First, that
change management works best if there is a clear, unequivocal need
for a company to do things differently, and that everyone understands the reasons behind the programme. Second, change
management is most effective when it involves the core of the

business and sets out to transform the organization fundamentally: in other words, when it involves everyone in one way or another. Perhaps there's another point to bear in mind here: you cannot get away with bullshit. If you try to pull the wool over people's eyes by fudging the real reasons for needing to change, then you simply generate cynicism and suspicion.

If you are anything like me, you are proud of the people who work in your company. You have set out to hire the best and to a large extent you probably think you've succeeded. They are smart; they are savvy. That's what you tell your customers.

So show them some respect! Don't fudge on the real reason why you need to change your organization, no matter how tough that message may be. If you are losing market share and your profitability is under threat, then explain to your people and help them understand why change is needed. By all means paint the vision of what you want to achieve in the most positive way possible and make them believe in it. But give it to them straight about the reasons for change.

The best way to beat the cynics and the nay-sayers is to be totally honest about the need for change.

KEY FACT

Change management demands honesty and commitment and it must pervade the very core of your business.

3   Changing cultures

'In the dead there is no change.'
Francis Bacon

It's tempting to see culture solely in terms of history. We think of cultures evolving slowly over time; we perceive the mix of art, tradition, customs, religion and folklore as all playing a part in the gradual development of a nation or a people's essential identity. You cannot design a programme to change these sort of cultures; you cannot even influence them very easily.

But you can change individual people and their attitude towards certain cultures, perhaps even their own.

Company culture is interesting. Sometimes, it's very strong and enormously positive. Take IBM, for example. The company's values are taken extremely seriously and everyone who works for 'Big Blue' learns to live by them. The culture feeds through to every aspect of the company's activity and it has clearly made a huge contribution to its success over the years. Indeed, many ex-IBMers carry on living those values long after they have left the firm.

But you get a different perspective on things when you look at the culture of a company like Enron. There, a negative culture of greed and cheating was allowed to spread through the company; indeed, it was encouraged by its senior management. In the end, of course, it brought about the company's downfall. OK, this is an extreme example, but we have all come across companies where a negative culture is obvious; where there seems to be a culture of laziness, blaming other people and departments for problems, clock-watching and time-serving and a lack of general interest in the organization and its customers.

People have a tendency to hide behind what they see as company culture rather than do anything to change it. And because few of us like change in the first place, we are happy to use company culture as an excuse to maintain the status quo. We have all heard people say things like 'Nice idea, but you'll never get the accounts people to run with it', or 'I can't see the IT department going along with this.'

In fact, what we should all be trying to create is a company culture with people at its heart. A culture in which people are motivated, respect each other, work hard, enjoy what they do and feel they are all playing a useful role in the success of their company.

But sadly these cultures are rarer than they should be. There are in fact many more types of negative culture. For example, there's the sort that developed at Enron, where greed and secrecy became prevalent. But far more common are cultures that grow up around outdated processes, working practices and values. In most cases they engender a solid resistance to change.

The main driving force of a company culture will usually be the way in which management decisions are taken and executed and how people at different levels in the organization relate to each other. So, for instance, in a role-based culture, process is very important and people will be unwilling to do things differently. In a status-based culture, everyone will know their place and be unwilling to step outside it. In an autocratic culture, where the leader is very powerful, decisions will be made as a result of his or her instructions and other people will not be used to making decisions for themselves.

Everyone else will adapt their behaviour according to the example set by those above them. Sometimes organizations that have been built up over a long period do things in a certain way, without being able to remember why. People within those organizations come to think that there is only one way to do things, accepting everything that they are told by those who create the company messages. The situation becomes self-perpetuating, and people simply reject any external intervention or fresh perspective.

The change manager must be able to define a culture fit for purpose. Appropriate cultures should be respected; but they can be enhanced and redirected through change management. Bad cultures need to be challenged at an early stage in the change management exercise can begin. It's also important to identify the supporters of negative cultures and understand their motives, before proceeding. This is all part of the process of risk assessment and planning.

Don't give long-established cultures too much respect; so often these can be smokescreens for low productivity, lack of motivation, old technology and out-of-date practices. It is even possible to change long-established cultures with an exciting new vision of the future and a rigorous plan for change.

KEY FACT

The best company cultures are properly designed; bad cultures tend to be those which have developed over many years of their own accord. People will often hide behind existing company cultures in order to resist change.

4   Changing the paradigm

'Change is not made without inconvenience, even from worse to better.'
Samuel Johnson

If it ain't broke, then don't fix it, the saying goes. And if it's generating big profits, then definitely don't fix it. Many companies create markets for themselves and then find bigger and better ways of doing business with those markets. They develop exactly the right products; they hone their sales and marketing, distribution systems and technology and just keep on milking the markets and watching their profits grow.

But the problem is that markets tend to change faster than most companies do. Furthermore, senior management who have built successful business models and have seen them perform well over long periods are invariably reluctant to make any fundamental changes. They might pull a few levers – often tactical measures – in response to a sudden deterioration in their market, but they will be unwilling to do anything more radical.

All companies have their own paradigms: their way of doing things. But successful companies develop particularly strong ones, usually driven by senior management. People start to believe that the company can do no wrong. So when things do turn sour, they find it almost impossible to accept that the paradigm needs to change. They cling on to the belief that if they make snap responses to market conditions – changing products, cutting costs, refocusing their sales operations – then profits will return.

There are plenty of examples. Look at the way the mobile phone industry was caught out by the sudden collapse in the market in 2001. Those companies that did not go bust will be hamstrung by massive corporate debt for years to come. Many of them simply refused to accept that they needed to change their corporate paradigm and so became victims of their own success.

The computer industry too is littered with similar stories. Many believed that the desktop computing boom would go on forever; that no matter what the prevailing economic conditions, companies would continue to upgrade systems and spend money on software and network technology. They had started to believe their own PR stories, that IT was now a non-negotiable cost item; companies simply had to keep increasing their investment in order to trade in the modern world. But things did not turn out like that. Across the world, businesses responded to the economic downturn by slashing spending on IT; they did not upgrade desktop systems; they postponed investment in networks and other IT infrastructures.

In successful companies, senior management often find it more difficult to change than anyone else. They take personal pride in their company cultures, their 'way of doing things', often going to great lengths to reinforce their people's belief in the status quo. Such managers find it especially hard to initiate major changes when things go wrong and they are forced into 'lever-pulling' tactical measures, such as immediate cost-cutting, in a bid to get everything back on track. The problem is exacerbated by the City which responds well to 'quick fixes' and does not like waiting to see the results of long-term change programmes. This simply plays into the hands of change-averse senior managers.

We have seen this particularly in the financial services industry, which has been notoriously slow to react to major changes in its markets. Many of the problems in the banking and insurance industry, for example, have come about as a result of a culture of lever-pulling and quick-fix solutions to deepseated problems which really require fundamental organizational, process and cultural change if they are to be solved.

However, senior management often find the prospect of major change deeply traumatic, regarding it as an admission of personal failure in the way they have led the company in the past. They can become swept up in the successful company paradigms they helped develop and lose sight of the markets in which they compete. Furthermore, they fail to understand that the more they keep faith with the old model in the face of adversity, and the more they resist change, the more they play into the hands of their people's natural unwillingness to do things differently. If those at the top of the company want to keep the status quo, then the majority of people beneath them will happily go along with the idea. No change is much easier than change. Senior managers must be change-orientated because their markets will always move faster than they can. They should avoid overcommitting themselves to any business paradigm simply because it appears to be working successfully. Sooner or later, it will need to change in line with the evolving needs of the market. Senior managers who put the notion of managed change at the heart of their company culture will always come out on top.

Perhaps the saying should be: even if it ain't broke, keep an open mind about how it can be improved.

KEY FACT

To be successful you must be a prophet of managed change and make it an essential part of your company ethos.

5   Change in three dimensions

'They always say time changes things, but actually you have to change them yourself.'
Andy Warhol

Ever tried erecting a tent in a howling gale? Even if you haven't, you can imagine how hard it must be. You get part of the frame up, then the tent starts blowing away. Then while you are grabbing hold of that, the frame falls over. You never quite know when the next gust is coming or where it's coming from. What seems like a simple job that could easily be tackled by a novice boy scout becomes a bit of nightmare, even for an experienced camper.

Running a change management project can be equally frustrating. What might seem like a straightforward programme, with easily achievable milestones, can be thrown into chaos by events which you could not predict or control.

The problem is that today every aspect of the market in which you operate has its own capacity for sudden change. There are countless forces of change buffeting businesses all the time: legislation (national and European); currency and economic fluctuations; technology and innovation; and market regulation, to name but a few. But perhaps the most difficult ones to deal with and anticipate are the speed at which companies can mount a competitive threat and the fickle nature of customers. Nothing stands still for a moment in either case, which is why they present change management leaders with a particular problem. On the one hand, they must appear firm about the need to change from position A to position B, and they must advocate passionately the benefits of making a major transformation. But on the other hand, they must be on the look-out for external events or shifts in market conditions that may impact on their change objectives, perhaps even invalidating them in the most extreme cases.

As we shall see, planning, leadership and communications are the linchpins of change management. People must understand why change is needed and feel that they are making progress at every stage in the change process. However, it's also the job of the change management leader to explain the three-dimensional nature of change, and point out that the programme may have to be redirected in response to many change factors which cannot be predicted at the start of the process.

You must take the time to explain to people that change management is not just a matter of setting a course and sailing from point A to point B. A few decades ago, when business, and perhaps life itself, was a little more predictable, the pace of change was much slower and the process of change was easier to manage. But now people need to know that change is a three-dimensional matter and can be unpredictable.

KEY FACT

People need to be introduced gradually to the idea of three-dimensional change. This is key to engendering the openmindedness and flexibility that you will need when you embark on your programme of change.

6 The benefit of a major crisis

'Only change the expiring flame renews.'
John Gay

Most people feel quite secure in their jobs. Provided we work hard, remain focused and use our experience and training, most of us normally remain reasonably confident about meeting our objectives. Remarkably few people actually lose their jobs because they underperform.

It's true of companies, too. They all go through good times and bad, and most go on to fight another day. Large-scale redundancies are actually quite rare, and corporate collapses usually result in a takeover with most employees transferring to the new parent company. The point is that the vast majority of working people and companies get through the ups and downs.

As a result, we all feel relatively comfortable most of the time. That's why we naturally resist corporate change; generally, we like things just the way they are.

So what's going to shake us out of our complacency and make us passionately embrace the idea of change? In short, nothing works quite like an immediate crisis. If we feel seriously threatened, then we are much more willing to accept the need for change.

When Barings faced total collapse following the losses incurred by rogue trader Nick Leeson, clearly nobody in the company was against the idea of change. The status quo was simply not an option; the bank had been brought to the brink of bankruptcy by inadequate risk management and internal controls. Change was imperative and everyone in the firm knew it.

But some crises are not so cut and dried. In the 1990s it became clear to many of Britain's high street banks that they too were facing a crisis. They were being threatened by competition from building societies which were demutualizing and turning themselves into banks. The incumbents were also being challenged by overseas banks moving into the UK market using new technology such as the Internet and telephone banking to reach customers. The old banks with their solid brands and expensive high street outlets had to change if they were to survive.

But this was no burning-platform situation. It was more like a smouldering platform as far as the vast majority of people in the banking industry were concerned. And it took them a long time to wake up to the seriousness of their situation. As a result, change was too slow and many banks are still paying the price.

If you face a crisis, even in the longer term, spell out all the grizzly details. Paint it black. Remember that successful change management demands honesty and frankness; but remember too that nothing motivates people to change better than a crisis. If you have one on your hands, then make good use of it.

KEY FACT

A crisis is the change manager's most powerful weapon. If you have one, happening now or gradually developing, then use it to the full.

7 The price of avoiding the culture of change

'A state without the means of some change is without the means of its conservation.'
Edmund Burke

Are you ready for change? Do you expect it any moment? Do you accept that you just don't know where or how you'll be working in even a year's time?

If you can answer 'yes' to all these questions and still maintain a total commitment to your current job, the processes you use and the people you work with, then you can count yourself as well equipped to make the most of the opportunities in today's business world. Congratulations! You are part of the culture of change. You understand that being proactively adaptable and open-minded are essential mental attributes in the early twenty-first century. You are a survivor.

But actually, we are talking about somebody else, aren't we? None of this applies to you or your company. I mean, things just don't change like that, do they? Not as far as you are concerned anyway. You don't need to change; you don't need to be part of this culture of change, whatever it is. You can see that it's probably a good thing, but it doesn't really affect you.

The latter attitude is much more common than the former. People know that the world is changing around them; they know that their customers and their markets are fluctuating and they understand that the pace of change is growing. But somehow they feel it simply does not involve them. They think it can go on around them and that they will not be affected by it.

Your challenge is to make people understand that the culture of change is the dominant one within your organization. They need to know that if they don't adopt it, then they are in a dwindling minority.

Many who work in the public sector, for example, find it hard to accept that the people in the communities they service are changing. Their customers' (the general public's) expectations of service, for example, are being driven higher by what they have grown used to in the private sector. And the gap in standards of service between, say, an online insurance broker and their local hospital is no longer acceptable to them. Many public-sector managers struggle with this notion.

You must get your people to become part of the culture of change. The whole process of change management will become easier if you do.

KEY FACT

The more you can convince your people that the culture of change will be permanent, the easier they will find change management. In the final analysis, most people are pragmatic.

8 Preparing for the journey

'The universe is change; our life is what our thoughts make it.'
Marcus Aurelius

Most of us have got used to the idea of international travel, and plane trips have long since lost their glamour. We like going away, especially if it's for a holiday in some exotic location, but the hassle and discomfort involved in getting there is always a bit of a downer.

Still, there are always ways of brightening up the journey. Keep the holiday brochure handy, so that the next time the man in the neighbouring seat starts snoring or steps on your toe on his second or third trip to the loo, you can look at the pictures of sun-drenched beaches and remind yourself why you are going though all this pain. Or you can reward yourself with a drink every thousand miles or so, watch a movie you have been meaning to see, and so on. Another way of cheering yourself up is to think what it would be like staying at home for two weeks in the drizzle. You could probably imagine nothing worse.

So what with the little treats along the way, the thought of the super hotel and beach awaiting you at your journey's end and occasional self-reminders about the weather you are leaving behind, the plane trip – even with the snores from the next seat – doesn't seem that bad. It'll be well worth it in the end, you decide.

Change management works in a pretty similar way. Generally, people don't like the journey, the process of change. It's uncomfortable, unsettling and sometimes downright unpleasant for them. It feels unnatural in the same way that some people feel that plane travel is not something we humans were designed for. Therefore, as a manager of change you need to act as 'pilot'.

That's why it's so important to sell the vision of the destination by giving them the colour brochure of where you are taking them with your change management journey. It helps them to blank out the discomforts of the travel process by remaining focused on all the benefits they will experience when they finally land.

Of course, you are there to make the journey as comfortable as you can. Celebrate milestones, make the journey as much fun as possible, and keep reminding your passengers how far you have travelled and how close you are to your journey's end.

As we shall see in later chapters, you must have a good crew. If you are piloting the plane, you cannot very well hand out the drinks, answer your passengers' questions and deal with complaints all at the same time. You need a team of people who are familiar with the journey and the detailed travel arrangements, and who know the destination well. It's important to surround yourself with an experienced team.

However, sometimes people are motivated to endure a long plane journey by what they are leaving behind. It's nice to think you are swapping the cold wind and rain of a typical English winter for a fortnight in the Caribbean. It certainly makes the plane journey feel less of a trial. But what if, like many refugees all over the world, you are leaving behind famine, war and abject poverty and heading for a new life in Western Europe or North America? You may know nothing about your destination or what it will hold for you; but you feel such a huge relief at escaping the misery of your homeland that you hardly care what happens to you when you reach your destination. Just being on that plane and getting away is all that matters. Never mind the discomforts of the journey – they certainly don't matter. This is a classic 'burning-platform' scenario. People simply must change, must go on that journey, if they are to survive, and they have to do it quickly before the platform is consumed by fire and they perish with it.

One of the key tasks for anyone driving a change management project is to assess what will motivate the passengers to make the journey in a positive way and contribute to its success. First, there's what they are leaving behind; second, there's the journey itself and what you are doing to make it as painless as possible; and third, there's the golden vision of the destination.

You must get this balance right. If the burning platform is roaring away, then that will drive your change programme. It's possible that people can't see that the platform they are standing on is on fire and you have to point it out to them. How many people noticed that Direct Line, with its telephone service, had ignited the platform of the traditional insurance industry before the flames were licking round the feet of the pin-striped brokers? Remember, too, how many retailers failed to see that their platform was being burned by the emergence of the big supermarket chains in the 1960s?

Even in a burning-platform situation you still need to show your people the destination brochure and tell them about the journey and how long it will take, although you know that you will have no trouble getting them on board your plane. On the other hand, if they are comfortable with the status quo, you know you are going to have to work very hard on selling your destination and making the journey both fun and painless.

Remember, it's your job to inspire your people to make the change management journey with you. You must work out in advance whether they are going to be motivated by what they are leaving or where they are going to; and don't forget that people hate the journey and will be disruptive unless they are motivated.

KEY FACT

Trust is an important driver for any change programme. People must believe you can navigate the journey successfully and get them there safely.

Part Two:
Planning and Launching your Change Programme

9   The timing of change management

'It's not that some people have willpower and some don't. It's that some people are ready to change and others are not.'
Dr James Gordon

You can always tell when a company which is embarking on a change management programme has not done its homework. The first sign is that the vision is woolly and non-specific. The second is that the timetable is too stretched. I have lost count of the number of change management programmes I have come across that were started with five-year objectives. Some of us might be dead by then.

The problem with long-term programmes is that they are almost bound to be affected by external events and developments within the market. For example, if you were an airline, all your plans would have been blown off course by the events of September 11, 2001. If you were an investment bank, your change management programme would have been shattered by the collapse in world financial markets in 2002.

Sometimes less dramatic developments can undermine change programmes, especially long-term ones. Technology, for example, can have a surprising impact. Look at the way the text-messaging phenomenon took off and is now being used by publishers, travel companies and broadcasters in a way that none of them could have predicted ten, or even five, years ago.

All change programmes must be set up in a way that allows them to be adapted to and accommodate unforeseen external events and circumstances. An essential element of this is the development of the culture of change within your organization. If people come to accept that being ready for change is a key part of working life, then they will take adjustments to the programme in their stride.

The vision should not change: that should be an absolute constant in any change process. However, the programme itself must be flexible enough to absorb and respond to external changes. And people involved in the programme must recognize how this might work right at the start of the process.

Even with this flexibility, long-term change programmes rarely work. People simply cannot relate to a vision if it is based on, say, a ten-year plan; their natural instinct is to imagine that they will probably not even be working with the company by then. Ideally, change management programmes should be based on a one- to three-year timeframe. The more you compress the process, the more it forces you to make your vision specific and to implement a detailed programme for achieving it. Clearly you don't want to shorten it so much that you risk failing to meet your objective; that would be a huge let-down for everyone involved and would damage people's confidence in the whole change management process. So give yourself enough time to meet your overall objective to deliver the vision.

If we accept that two of the key elements of any change management programme are the vision and the process, then right behind them come the milestones. It's especially important for anyone involved in a change management process to feel that they are making progress towards the achievement of the vision. On a typical one- to three-year programme, this means having at least quarterly milestones and reviews.

Let's go back to the analogy of the plane journey in the previous chapter. We talked about how passengers need to know how the journey is going, how far they have gone and how much longer it will be before their destination. If you recall, we explained the need for cabin staff – the people managing the change process rather than leading it (that was the pilot, you'll remember) – to answer their questions, keep them focused on the journey and make them aware of the progress they were making.

Milestones needn't be complex. But they are an opportunity to bring people together to celebrate specific progress within the programme. They also give you a chance to review the programme as a whole, and take into account any external developments or events. Additionally, they present you with an opportunity to re-motivate people and keep them focused on the vision. Milestone events also give the vision leader the chance to reinforce her commitment.

Milestones can and should include different sorts of measures. For instance, on one level, they should encompass measures such as volumes of people who have received particular training; or the number of seats filled at a call centre; or the departments now 'live' on a new piece of technology. Milestones can also involve attitudinal research. For example, if one of the goals of the change programme is to improve customer relations, it is relatively easy to assess progress by comparing research at the start of the process with the same exercise undertaken after, say, one year.

However, milestones must include proper financial measures. Is the programme increasing revenues, expanding the customer base or cutting costs? Senior management who support the funding for the programme will want to see evidence that it is producing a good Return On Investment (ROI). More on that later.

You can make as much or as little of your milestone events as you wish. Personally, I think they are always great for internal PR, and I believe that particular efforts and achievements by individuals within the programme should be publicly rewarded.

KEY FACT

Change management works best if it's based on a one- to three-year programme with milestones every three to six months.

10   Creating a crystal-clear vision

'We all have big changes in our lives that are more or less a second chance.'
Harrison Ford

When Moses announced that he would lead his people from Egypt, he promised that he would take them to the land of milk and honey. As everyone knows, the journey was very long and fraught with problems, but Moses just about succeeded in keeping the Israelites together. He succeeded for three good reasons. First, they were leaving behind a 'burning platform'. There was no future for them in Egypt and Moses' people knew that. Second, they bought the vision of the land of milk and honey. It sounded fantastic and they could see how it would be far better there than it had been to date for them in Egypt. And third, and most important, they had confidence both in Moses to lead them there successfully and that the discomforts of the journey would be worth it in the end.

Having convinced people of the need to change, the vision is the crucial element in any change programme. This is the thing that is going to inspire you and your people to make the transformation successfully.

But what makes a good vision? So many change management projects fail because the vision is weak, too abstract or so ambitious that it simply looks unachievable.

Let's look at some examples. One company I have dealt with set itself the goal of 'Becoming the number one accounting software company in the world within five years'. OK, the vision had merit in that it was ambitious, bold and specific. But, given that the company concerned had a tiny market share and a very modest presence in the United States, nobody bought the vision. It seemed an impossible goal and was therefore not credible.

Another company set out its vision for change to become 'Totally customer-focused'. This was an organization that had recently been privatized and was attempting to compete in the free market for the first time. The vision was of course laudable. But what did it mean? People in the company already knew that they had to learn to become more customer-focused. This seemed more like a cultural or communications strategy rather than a vision. It failed because people simply didn't see it as a vision.

When Arsene Wenger took over as manager of Arsenal Football Club, he arrived at the end of a barren period for the London club. The directors and the fans were hungry for success. For them, the 'burning platform' was jogging along in the upper half of the Premiership and winning a trophy every now and again. This was never going to be enough.

After a few weeks at Highbury, Wenger set out his vision. He wanted Arsenal to become one of the dominant clubs in Europe, challenging for honours at every level and winning trophies on a regular basis. He explained that to do this he would be looking for players from all over the world, not just the UK. The fans would have to show some patience while he set about his change programme, he explained. And the Arsenal board would have to dig deep into their reserves to enable him to put his plan into practice.

Wenger's vision was ambitious but credible. He explained what the club would need to do to make this vision a reality and the sacrifices that would be needed. Favourite players were sold, and new ones – some of them complete unknowns – were brought in. The fans and the board kept faith with Wenger because they believed in the vision and his ability to bring it about. They liked his honesty, his cool intelligence and his tendency not to gloss over difficulties; they were prepared to give him the time he needed to deliver results. After two doubles (FA Cup and Premiership trophies) in three years and a further FA Cup triumph, Wenger is well on his way to achieving his vision.

Leaving aside Wenger's obvious quality as a football manager, his vision was a masterpiece. It was exciting, ambitious, believable and specific. He carried the fans, the club directors, the players and the media with him as he took Arsenal forward. Your change management vision must do the same thing. Don't bury it in meaningless corporate or marketing jargon. Make it exciting. Use appealing language. (What could be more enticing than the idea of the land of milk and honey?) But above all else make it believable. And then lead from the front.

KEY FACT

Change management visions must be exciting, precise and believable. People rarely respond well to vague or 'obvious' goals.

11 Planning ahead of the change curve

'There is nothing like returning to a place that remains unchanged to find the ways in which you yourself have altered.'
Nelson Mandela

When SmithKline Beckam and Beecham carried out the first transatlantic merger in the pharmaceutical industry, the boards of both companies knew exactly what they wanted to achieve with the deal. They set out to create a new major global company from two second-tier enterprises.

The change programme involved no less than 200 teams focused on building a new company, with its own unique culture, from the foundations of SKB and Beechams.

The process took the best part of five years to complete and is generally regarded as a model of change management excellence. Little did they know that they would be going through the whole exercise again a few years later when the combined group was merged with Glaxo to create a pharmaceutical giant.

But how often do you hear of two companies being thrown together by an agreement between major shareholders without the slightest thought being given to change management? All the focus is on short-term issues such as market share, product synergies and possible savings, and yet the real shareholder value is bound to be governed by how well the two companies are merged operationally and culturally.

Once the short-term benefits have been used up, many mergers falter because of the lack of change management planning. Think of all the takeovers in the utility sector as the markets deregulated: electricity companies merged with water boards, which in turn teamed up with the gas suppliers. Then came the American utility groups and the big European players, all keen to grab a slice of the UK market. Of course the business logic and short-term benefits of these deals were compelling to shareholders at the time, but change management hardly got a look in. A good many of these deals turned sour, not just because market conditions changed, but also because the management teams of the merged companies were not sufficiently integrated to handle tougher market conditions.

There are two points that need to be made here. First, change management is a major factor in the delivery of long-term shareholder value. It should be a boardroom issue right at the start of any merger discussion. You need a vision of the sort of company you are trying to create through the merger. It may be that you don't want to build a new company, but rather you want to bring one company under the control and culture of another. Fine. But whatever the case, you need a vision, an agreement on the change management objectives and a programme for achieving these at the time of the announcement of the merger. When you bring two companies together, you change them both. If you plan for that change, you will stand a good chance of delivering long-term shareholder value.

The second point is that if you fail to put change management on the agenda at the time of a merger you are taking multiple, unnecessary risks. If, as happened in the UK's utility industry, the market conditions suddenly change, newly merged companies often struggle. By then it may be too late for a conventional programme of change to be fully effective, and your merged company may become overwhelmed by market dynamics before it has time to adjust. If you lose control of the relationship between your company and the market, then managed change becomes extremely difficult. Often, in these circumstances, something more radical may be required, such as a sale or a further merger.

One final word on this particular point: remember that change management is not just for big companies when they merge; there are just as many challenges and issues when you bring together two small companies. The risks and rewards are the same.

KEY FACT

When companies are merged, effective management of change can deliver long-term shareholder value. But to do this, you must start the process early by agreeing the vision, the objectives and the programme before the merger is finalized.

12   Being blind to the past

'Change your thoughts and you change your world.'
Norman Vincent Peale

Self-honesty is a problem in many large companies. People find it hard to face the truth about themselves and their organization, especially when things are going wrong. Revenues and profits may be down, the share price may be under siege and customers may be deserting the company by the score, but that may not stop managers telling their people that everything is going to turn out just fine. They will always be willing to talk about their strategies for putting the company back on the road to recovery. However, they rarely offer much public or detailed analysis of how the company's problems were created in the first place. That's nearly always left to people outside the company.

Marconi is a case in point. During the build-up to the company's debt crisis in 2002, the directors found it hard to accept that the problems stemmed mainly from strategic decisions made by the board, rather than deteriorating trading conditions in some of their key markets. When you are close to the coalface, and under pressure from shareholders, it's natural to lay blame anywhere other than your own door.

The same was true at Marks & Spencer during its problem period in the late 1990s. All the senior management told its people and the City was that the company would return to profitability. In the end it did, but it was nothing like as soon as the optimists at Marks & Spencer's head office had predicted. And even then it only came about as the result of a major programme of change, initiated by a new team of directors.

Many senior managers find it impossible to put anything other than a rosy glow on their companies' prospects. They might argue that it is their job to lead and motivate and therefore they must be positive; and besides, they would say, they are in the business of building confidence in the company's shares. And, of course, we all want to be associated with solutions rather than problems.

However, there is a clear line to be drawn between the way senior managers should communicate in these circumstances with external audiences such as the City, customers and suppliers, and the approach they take with their own people. Naturally, they want to put the best possible spin on the company's prospects to the external audiences, but they must be totally honest with their own employees if they want them to accept the need for change and then buy in to a specific programme.

Successful change management demands total self-honesty. The people at the top of a failing company must be prepared to go public – internally at least – on the root causes of their problems. The dirty washing must come out of the basket, and everyone in the company must be shown it. Then people will see the need for fundamental change. That doesn't mean doing away with senior management's positive vision and expressions of belief that the company is on the road to recovery – in many ways that helps the change management process, but only if it's backed by rigorous and honest internal analysis of the company's problems.

KEY FACT

People dislike change. If you give them half a chance they will avoid it. If you want their commitment you must be honest and open about your company's problems and how they can be resolved.

13 Bite-size change management

Sometimes there is an unavoidable gap between the vision and what your organization is capable of achieving through a change management programme. For example, you may have a vision to become a top-ten software company, or even 'the world's favourite airline'. But people can see that it's going to take more than a single change management programme to achieve that shining vision.

So what should you do? Downgrade the vision, perhaps; come up with a less ambitious one that your people will feel is more realistic and attainable? Actually, that's not always necessary. Sometimes it pays to have a big, long-term goal that excites and motivates everyone in the organization, even though they know that it is going to take several change programmes and a whole range of initiatives and investments to get there.

Once again, it comes down to the importance of honesty and clarity in change management. Stick with the big vision, but be clear about exactly how far each of your change programmes is going to take your organization towards the ultimate goal.

Be specific about the objective of the programme and take care to explain why it can only take you so far towards the vision. People will want to know about the constraints you are working under and will need to understand, in general terms, what else has to happen before the vision can be delivered. If the vision is a long-term one and everyone in the organization is aware of that, it is perfectly reasonable to have several self-contained change management programmes over a number of years in order finally to achieve the ultimate goal. You may well need subsidiary visions for each of these programmes in order to keep people focused, but take care to ensure that they relate closely to the overall long-term goal.

British Airways, for example, had to go through a series of programmes of change before it went live with its claim of being 'the world's favourite airline'. Everything from routes, pricing, design, cabin and ground service had its own change management programme. However, everyone involved knew that these programmes were all staging posts on the road towards the achievement of the ultimate goal.

KEY FACT

Big, lighthouse visions sometimes involve several change programmes. It's critical to tell people about why you cannot achieve the overall vision in one go. It's all part of the process of gaining their confidence.

14   Changing when things are going well

'Turbulence is life-force. It is opportunity. Let's love turbulence and use it for change.'
Ramsay Clark

Given people's natural reluctance to change in the first place, they find it doubly difficult to accept it when things seem to be going well and there is no obvious reason for upheaval. This is the opposite end of the spectrum from the burning platform, the extreme crisis which everyone can see poses a serious and immediate threat. If they cannot understand or relate to the driver for change, then they will find it hard to accept that there's a need to change.

However, it's when things are going well, with revenues climbing and profits growing steadily, that you can make the most effective and creative changes. Rather than simply respond to market pressures when they arise, your ability to drive change in the good times will allow you to anticipate the needs of the market and give you a competitive advantage.

Let's look at an example. You run a high street chain specializing in low-cost electrical goods. You are coming to the end of your second record year in succession and your people have enjoyed good bonuses and above-inflation salary increases. However, your margins are tight and you depend on volume to meet your shareholders' expectations. Your research has indicated that the upward pressure on commercial rents is building fast in many of the towns and cities where you have leasehold premises. More than half your sites are facing a rent review within three years. Furthermore, there are indications that the cycle of low interest rates might be coming to an end; any rate increase would impact on your revenues.

Your board has decided to reduce its presence on the high street and to expand its online sales business. This will mean closing several stores and retraining for many employees who will be offered jobs at a new customer contact centre. At the same time, the company is going to be rebranded.

Your people's reaction is likely to be one of disbelief. They will want to know why on earth the company wants to put them through all this when things are going so well.

If you want their buy-in to this programme of change and through it give your company a powerful competitive advantage in the medium term, then you have to give your people the full story. It goes back to what I said before: honesty is the best policy. Don't hide behind a 'Don't worry about it. We know what's good for you' façade. Tell them, in detail, why you want to bring about this change. More important still, explain to them how they will benefit from the anticipation of changes in market conditions.

The onus will be on you to communicate your ideas, your reasons for driving the changes and the opportunities for everyone when you achieve your goal. It's always easier to bring about change in troubled times, but it's potentially much more valuable if you can pull it off when business is good.

KEY FACT

Change management is hardest when organizations seem to be performing well. People find it hard to relate to problems they cannot see.

15 Keeping in touch with customer expectations

'Only the wisest and stupidest of men never change.'
Confucius

If you went to buy a new car today, you'd be surprised if you were offered one that had manual windows or didn't have central locking. If you ordered a new telephone, you would be appalled if the phone company said it would not be able to deliver it for six weeks or so. In the same way, we expect quick service in restaurants, clothes that don't shrink in the wash and computers and televisions that always work when you turn them on.

Now let's go back twenty years or so. Yes, it was frustrating being told you had to wait for your telephone to be delivered; it was faintly annoying to have so little gadgetry in your car included in the price; we tolerated slow service in restaurants because it was the norm; and we simply accepted that electrical goods of all sorts – especially computers – were complicated and unreliable.

For all this, we didn't complain about poor goods and services any more than we do now. It's simply that our standards and expectations have risen dramatically with the relentless growth of the economy, industrial globalization and the ubiquity of international brands which have established new norms for the quality of goods and services around the world.

But did you notice this happening? When did you become aware that your expectations had moved on from where they had been?

That's the problem that many organizations face. They find it hard to track their customers' expectations of them and, as a result, cannot keep up with the pace of change.

Take Royal Mail as an example. As part of a monopoly it was naturally not as customer-sensitive as it might have been as a private company; but for many years it seemed completely oblivious to the fact that its customers were increasingly disappointed in the levels of service they received. It raised its prices time and time again; and on every occasion it blamed rising costs. Royal Mail's management seemed not to recognize that it was necessary to go on improving its service in order to justify the price increases. It just expected its customers to pay because it had failed to manage its costs.

Many of the private rail operators suffer from the same problem. They have simply not kept pace with their customers' need for a reliable, safe and clean transport service.

But at the other end of the spectrum, some companies have not only met their customers' expectations, they have actually set out to gain their loyalty by exceeding their needs and, indeed, have set new standards for service in their markets. Some of the major credit card firms, for example, have done this by offering free insurance, air miles, discounts, wine clubs, telephone services and other benefits.

New companies, often quite small ones, create space for themselves in established markets simply by offering a better, cheaper or faster service. Look at the whole online stockbroking phenomenon: tiny companies which quickly won significant market share from the traditional players. And then there are the no-frills airlines that have changed the whole shape of the short-haul market.

It's not so much customers' changing expectations that confound many companies; it's the pace of change and their inability to respond to it that really throws them. If you can instil a culture of change in your organization, it will enable you to become both much more responsive to changes in customer expectations and more sensitive to the gathering pace of change in the wider marketplace.

KEY FACT

Customers drive markets. Their expectations of you are growing all the time. If you can introduce a culture of change in your organization, you will become much more sensitive and responsive to the changing needs of your customers.

16   Change due to competition

> 'We live in a moment in history where change is so speeded up
> that we begin to see the present only when it is already
> disappearing.'
> R.D. Laing

We all know that companies that stand still start to die. Perhaps we can go one stage further than that by saying that, these days, companies that don't change fast enough also put themselves under threat.

Competitive advantage is driven by a company's ability to see an opportunity and then enable the organization to respond to it at the right time.

A typical example might be the need to build a call centre in order to match the level of service provided by a competitor. The existence of new technology might be the driving force here, when it provides the means for a company to work much more efficiently than before, and so supply a better service for customers. But the company must manage the change process well to make the best use of the technology and get the timing right. If it fails on either count, it not only allows its competitors to maintain the advantage, but also starts to lose market share. And while that is happening, the competitor may be driving up the standard of service still further, making the task of catching up even more of a challenge.

In the past there may have been room for small sleepy companies to keep doing things the way they always had because they had a loyal and regular customer base. But these days, blind loyalty is a luxury few of us can afford. Loyalty has to be earned through premium service, pricing or outstanding product quality. Likewise, large companies that used to rely simply on the fact that everyone knew their name can no longer be so complacent. The plethora of channels between the suppliers and customers – retail outlets, the Internet, catalogues, resellers and partners, to name but a few – allows customers much greater opportunity to find companies offering better products and better services at better prices than many of the big brands.

Look what's happened in the market for CDs and books. People don't think twice about comparing prices at HMV or W.H. Smith with what they can find on the Internet. Sometimes the savings are tiny; but that doesn't matter: the big benefit of shopping for goods such as books and CDs on the Internet is that it's much more convenient and efficient than visiting the high street.

Brand, of course, is still a major differentiator, and companies will always invest heavily in their names and what they stand for in the market. But the march of technology is changing the relationship between companies and their customers. The opportunity to use technology and new ways of doing business – such as using contact centres – to challenge established brand loyalties and values is growing all the time.

Look at the way First Direct, the first telephone bank, succeeded in taking business away from the traditional high street players by offering customers a new kind of service. First Direct's timing, its judgement about how customers' needs and expectations had changed, was spot on. The Internet, and the way that new companies build markets for themselves simply by doing things differently, is also rich with similar examples.

What is undoubtedly the key factor in today's battle for customers is the speed at which an organization can respond to change or to a new opportunity. If you can meet customers' needs before anyone else, then you clearly have a commercial advantage. Once again, competitive edge, like so many other key drivers in today's business world, largely depends on your organization's ability to change and change fast. If you have a culture of change in your company, you are much more likely to be able to maintain your advantage than one that still treats change as a special event.

KEY FACT

Competitive advantage is all about being able to change quickly. If you create a culture of change, the whole process becomes faster and more effective.

17   When whole organizations face change

'If we don't change, we don't grow. If we don't grow, we aren't really living.'
Gail Sheeh

When the Conservative government first announced its plans to privatize British Rail, you would have struggled to find a single person in the organization who supported the idea. The same was true of the old water and electricity boards. There is also plenty of evidence of anxiety and lack of support among private-sector employees when companies become involved in takeovers.

You also come across entire organizations that refuse to adopt certain new technologies. Some regional newspaper groups in the 1970s and early 1980s, for example, publicly stated that they would not introduce direct input technology, largely as a way of appeasing the print unions and avoiding industrial unrest.

The minute that senior management gives the slightest impression that they are resisting change, then the entire organization underneath them falls into line. As I have said before, everybody is comfortable with the status quo and all it takes is a signal from the top that 'change is bad' or even that 'change is not necessarily good' and it becomes company gospel. And the further down the organization you go, the more fervent people become in their resistance to change.

But when senior managers want to bring about change, they face the reverse problem. They have to shout it from the rooftops if they want anyone in their organization to listen. There is no doubt that many organizations fail to change when they need to do so because senior management simply ducks the issue. First, many of them have no idea how to initiate or handle major corporate change; and second, they may themselves be frightened by the whole idea. For many senior managers, it's a risk they do not need to take: why rock the boat when they may have only a few years to go before they move on to their next role or retire? And who can blame them?

It certainly takes courage for a senior manager, perhaps a chief executive officer (CEO), to lead massive organizational change, because it may demand uncomfortable honesty. For example, the CEO must be prepared to make an immediate break with the past, draw a line in the sand and focus the company on the path towards a vision of the future. In doing so, the CEO must distance him- or herself from the past without actually denigrating the people involved. Of course, people need to understand what needs to change and why before they can accept the need for a change programme. But don't dwell on the past; you will get the best out of people if you can keep them focused on the future and the opportunities that will open up to them as the change programme progresses.

Once people understand the need to change, the next challenge is to get them to buy your vision and to carry them with you. Chapters 18–26 will lay out the ground rules for making this happen, showing how you make everyone in your company embrace change willingly and see the advantages of it for themselves, their colleagues and their customers.

KEY FACT

Breaking with your immediate past is an essential first step towards helping your people understand the need for change.

18 Risk analysis and management

> *'If your time to you is worth savin' then you better start
> swimming or you'll sink like a stone, for the times they are
> a-changin'.'*
> Bob Dylan

All change management projects carry significant risk, which needs
to be balanced against the risk attached to not going ahead with the
programme and maintaining the status quo. Not infrequently the
latter risk is greater than the former, so that in such circumstances
change itself becomes a risk mitigator.

However, risk analysis for the change programme is important.
You must look at every aspect of your programme and evaluate
where the greatest risks of failure lie, and the cost of those failures
in terms of damage to the overall programme and real impact on
the company's bottom line. And you must use this information to
shape and inform your programme.

The key areas for risk analysis are

- failure to meet milestones, which might cause the programme to
  be extended or changed
- external factors that could blow the programme off course or
  undermine it
- loss of key members of the change management team
- loss of vision leader or leaders (i.e. programme sponsor and
  'lighthouse')
- threats to funding
- sudden collapse in support from top management
- slippage in support of key participants in the change programme.

As mentioned earlier, certain steps can be taken to reduce many
of these risks. For example, the funding for the programme must be
secured for the duration of the programme and protected from the
threat of annual review. However, you cannot eliminate all risks
surrounding the budget: the company or organization might suddenly be faced with a major crisis which would force the budget to
be cut, no matter what.

These days, risk management is an important corporate function, through which companies protect their shareholders, customers, suppliers and employees from the full impact of unexpected events or things not going according to plan. Change management programmes need all the analysis and risk planning that would be afforded to key corporate activities like research and development and key product launches.

Having analysed all the factors that might threaten the success of the programme, the next step is to work out strategies for dealing with them. What would you do, for example, if your leader – the person who 'owns' the programme – suddenly left your organization? What steps would you take to minimize the damage?

All the risks need solutions worked out in advance. You then need to look at specific nightmare scenarios. What would you do if, say, two or even more of those problem events occurred at the same time? Again, you mitigate this risk by having a plan of action that can be immediately deployed.

Risk management is a key element of change management because so much will be riding on the project's success. But even more significant is that once you embark on a change programme you have, in a sense, created a burning platform for yourself. There is no way back to the status quo once you have started down this road. So it must be made to work. That's why managing the risks surrounding your programme of change is so important.

KEY FACT

Risk analysis and risk management are as important as the programme of change itself. Unless you know your risks and have plans for dealing with them, the whole programme could fail, and fail badly.

19   Leading and managing the process

'I don't drop players. I make changes.'
Bill Shankly

There is a big difference between leading the change process and directing its implementation. Sometimes you come across highly energetic chief executives who can combine both functions, but they are a rarity. It is also a risky strategy, because CEOs obviously have many other priorities and can be drawn into focusing on major issues or problems to the exclusion of almost everything else. As a result, the programme is suddenly thrown over to other people who may know little or nothing about change management or the progress of the programme.

Tempting though it may be for CEOs to take charge of the change process, it's far better for them to be focused on owning the vision and leading the programme, and leaving the management of the process to a separate team. Being 'vision-master' is pretty demanding: the CEO has to be seen to be selling the big idea the whole time and all his actions and words must be compatible with the change programme. He also needs to be acutely aware of any problems within the process itself, so that he can lend his weight to fixing them and reinforcing the vision whenever needed. Although he must be seen to be leading the vision and to be the embodiment of it, he also needs direction from the change management team about when to say what about the programme and to whom. As the public face of the vision, he is the programme's most important asset, which is another argument for separating the two functions of leadership and management.

Henry Wendt, the CEO of SmithKline Beckan, and Robert Bauman, CEO of Beecham, took joint responsibility for owning the change management vision when their companies were merged. It was a complex picture involving the development of a powerful new joint culture known as 'simply better', based on 'continuous improvement through continuous learning'. On a practical level, that meant a huge international exercise enabling the two companies to share information contained on their databases. Given that pharmaceutical companies are basically knowledge-based businesses, this would have been a huge undertaking.

The CEOs played a key role in selling the vision both internally and externally. Although they took no practical part in the work of over 200 global change management teams, they understood the programmes in enormous detail. They could answer questions on the precise status of the change management process, and kept themselves informed of problems. As they went round the company, they not only maintained people's focus on the vision, they were also able to demonstrate that they were completely in touch with the process. Now, that really is change management leadership.

The change management team should be made up of people who understand not only the programme, the process and the milestones; they must also understand and be sensitive to the current company culture. In other words, the people who are going on the change journey need to be able to relate to the change management team as 'their own'. But you may also need some external expertise – change management consultants – to help you manage the process. It's important that these people are kept behind the scenes if possible, with full-time company people taking the front-line roles when the programme actually gets going. Consultants are most effective when they are involved in putting the plan together rather than actually leading its implementation.

Once again, it boils down to trust. People are much more likely to buy into a change management programme if it is run by familiar faces. There is nothing more unnerving than being briefed on a change programme and then being confronted with having to deal with a team of external consultants hired to bring it about. People will be suspicious and unsettled, suspecting that consultants have nothing to lose personally if the change programme fails. They will be much more inspired being led through the programme by managers who are driven by the need for a successful outcome.

KEY FACT

The leadership and the management of change roles are best kept separate. Keep the CEO focused on leadership and have a separate change team led by people familiar with the company's current culture and objectives.

20 When to use change management consultants

'There are two kinds of people: those who are changing and those who are setting themselves up to be changed.'
Jim Clemmer

One of the problems of managing change is that it involves skills outside those normally needed in the day-to-day operational running of an organization. And given that you cannot afford to risk your change management programme failing, sometimes you have no option but to seek help from specialist consultants.

First, a word of warning. 'Change management' means different things to different people, and there are plenty of less than effective management consultancy firms offering themselves as process-change specialists without having the necessary track-record. If you are trying to minimize your risk of failure by involving a firm of outside consultants, you want to be sure you are getting the real McCoy. Look for clear evidence of major change management projects that have been fully documented and, ideally, authenticated by a third party. And remember to review the cvs of the individual consultants who are put forward by your chosen firm.

There is a strong case for involving consultants at the early stages of the planning and development of the change programme. As mentioned before, the vision is the key component of the programme. External consultants can provide valuable help over the definition of the vision. Being outsiders, they will feel free to challenge senior management rather than accept their ideas without question. It's important for the vision to be challenged, tested and amended until it's right, and consultants are often well placed to carry out this task in collaboration with senior management.

There's also a key role for consultants to play in talking to employees to find out about the true nature of the company's culture, discussing how they feel about processes, their managers, colleagues and other departments. In this context people tend to open up far more to external consultants than they would to their own colleagues or people from another department. It is very important to discover the true state of your organization before developing your change management plan. So this early internal research is an ideal job for consultants.

The third area where consultants are particularly useful is in the development of the change management plan itself. Good consultants are able to bring years of experience to the process and will know where all the major challenges and obstacles are hidden. They should also be able to advise on the timetable for the programme, develop achievable milestones and assist with the whole process of keeping people motivated as the programme progresses. Indeed, there is often a case for consultants remaining involved throughout the programme.

However, in my view, it's important not to involve consultants in the frontline delivery of the change programme. People want the vision to come from their own leaders, not an external person. Equally, they feel most comfortable dealing with people they know and who are going to be directly affected by the outcome of the programme.

Finally, be warned that consultants can be extremely expensive and are adept at 'mission creep'. One way to control the expense is to choose a consultancy that would be willing to share the risk with you. If, for instance, you have defined a level of revenue growth that you want to achieve over the next three years, you could offer to pay the consultants a percentage of that growth if they will work with you over that period. Not every firm will be willing to take such a risk themselves; and their reluctance may help you eliminate them as a possible partner. If they don't believe that their involvement is going to produce dramatic results, would you want to be working with them anyway?

Change management carries inherent risk. If you can minimize it by involving consultants and getting them to share in the residual risk, then you give yourself the best possible chance of making your programme a success.

KEY FACT

Consultants are best kept for the elements of the programme where they can add most value, rather than being allowed to take over the whole exercise. The vision and communications should be run by your own people.

21   Return on investment (money)

'Only I can change my life. No one can do it for me.'
Carol Burnett

These days, few companies even consider investing in technology or management consultancy without seeing Return On Investment (ROI) figures in advance. And change management is no exception.

Some people struggle with the very idea of having to demonstrate that the company will get a decent ROI from a change programme. They will talk about it being a long-term investment, one that is simply impossible to quantify. But I think it's important to grasp the nettle and develop your ROI case. Programmes of change can involve huge budgets, and they must earn a return.

Part of the ROI calculation is straightforward. Will your programme deliver a reduction in costs? For instance, if it involves the introduction of new technology, much of that may be a capital investment which can be written off over several years. However, the technology will almost certainly involve new processes and need fewer people to carry them out. You can therefore look at your year-on-year savings in people costs against the investment in the IT, spread over perhaps five years or longer. A reduction in headcount may mean you need less office space; perhaps you can vacate a few floors or even an entire building. That yields immediate additional savings in rent, rates and services, which will impact on this year's profit and loss account.

Another part of the ROI calculation can focus on productivity gains, perhaps giving you more service capacity to sell to customers. Or the gain may feed through to product development if you are a manufacturer for instance, giving you more goods to sell.

A third calculation could be based around improvements in customer service. Some might suggest that you cannot apply a numerical value to this, but I would argue that you can and you should. If customer service is improving, then you are making a contribution to customer retention and loyalty. That feeds through to a reduction in customer losses and helps create a framework for additional sales to current customers. A simple piece of qualitative research will give you some raw data in both these fields from which you can extrapolate a wider picture.

If you cannot justify your change management project in financial terms, then you will always struggle to get it approved and supported, especially when the economic conditions are tough. And remember that the more difficult the climate, the more finance directors will be focused on short-term returns.

KEY FACT

Return On Investment calculations will help to make the case for a major change management programme.

22   Return on investment (people)

'Change is the constant, the signal for rebirth, the egg of the phoenix.'
Christina Baldwin

Imagine that you have been in your current job for about six years following a promotion. You used to work in a room with six others, but now you have your own office, which you like. You feel you work hard for about eight hours a day, but you like to get away at 5.30 p.m. sharp. Happily, you work just a hundred yards from the station and you are usually home by 6.20 p.m. (by then it's still light enough for a game of tennis or some gardening in the summer). You enjoy your job and your working conditions and feel that you are rewarded adequately rather than generously.

You have got used to working at a certain pace and in a certain way. You have quite a lot of contact with customers and they seem to be happy with the service you provide. You don't have much involvement with people outside your department, but that doesn't bother you because all they tend to do when you come across them is interfere with your day-to-day work. You prefer to be left alone to get on with your job.

Suddenly you're told that everything is going to change. Your company has launched what the management call its 'Winning Back the Customer' programme. On the face of it, this sounds like a good idea. The Chief Executive says he is leading a drive to win back 5,000 customers within five years. He says he believes the company could triple its sales if it succeeded.

Great. Well, not that great actually, as far as you are concerned. As part of this so-called programme, you are going to have to do the following:

- give up your office and go and work in what they call an 'open' environment
- get used to working in a completely new department (yours is being merged with two others)
- move to a different building on the other side of town

- be prepared to start work earlier and finish later, if required (though you still end up working the same sort of hours as you do now)
- learn how to use a new computer system
- deal with a whole load of new customers – many more than you are used to handling.

You feel hugely demotivated. You are being asked to give up your own office, which you thought was part of your promotion. Your journey to and from work is going to be much more difficult. Your hours are less predictable. What's more, you have got to learn a new computer system while your entire job has changed. 'If this is change management then they can keep it', you think.

This scenario is not untypical. Our hypothetical middle manager's world has been turned upside down. She likes the vision, but not at that price.

What's gone wrong here? The simple answer is that nobody has pointed out the personal benefits of the programme to this manager. She has been told, in some detail, how everything is going to change, and in general terms – in so far as it all relates to the vision – she can see why the changes are necessary.

But something really important is missing. Nobody has told her what's in it for her. How is this going to benefit her? All she can see are disadvantages. The office of her own that she worked so hard for is disappearing; her hours are going to be less predictable (better cancel the membership at the local tennis club); she is moving to a new building miles from her station; she has got to learn a new computer system; and rub shoulders with a bunch of people she has never met before, in an open-plan office!

Yet there are benefits for her, if only someone bothered to share them with her. For a start, she is going to learn some important new skills which will make her much more marketable and enhance her career. Furthermore, when she completes her training she will be given a bonus and there will be rewards for meeting customer satisfaction targets. Yes, her hours are changing, but then she is going to be offered a flexible benefits package, which means she can decide whether she wants a company car, more pension or longer holidays. Her flexibility is being rewarded by more choice on how she is paid.

And there's more. Her open-plan office will have proper air conditioning (which she has never had before) and access to a subsidized restaurant and company gym.

Just as it's important to put across the ROI message about a change programme to the finance director, so you have to sell the personal benefits to every single person in the organization. That's their ROI.

KEY FACT

People can be as sceptical about change programmes as the stereotypical finance director. You need to sell the personal benefits of the programme to your people in just the same way you have to sell the ROI to the board.

23 Effective communication

'Affirmations are like prescriptions for certain aspects of yourself you want to change.'
Anon

Few people who have had anything to do with change management would deny that communications is a key discipline. You can train people, brief them and change their benefits packages until you are blue in the face; but unless you communicate *with* them, your change management programme will be slow to move forwards.

But let's be clear what we mean by communications. It's a two-way process. It only works if you engage in a dialogue with people, listening to them as well as talking to them.

Half the problem with corporate communications, especially that directed at internal audiences, is that it is too one-way focused. Senior management are generally good at 'putting their message across' but they can be poor at proper communications.

So often this is because the mechanisms for people to feed back their own thoughts, ideas and reactions to what they are being told are far too limited. We have all been to company meetings where there's a long presentation by a manager and then at the end of it he says: 'Right then. Any questions?' Silence. This must surely be the most intimidating environment possible for anyone to venture an opinion, give feedback or ask a question. People worry that they may upset their boss by giving an honest view, or they think they will sound stupid by asking a question. Much safer to keep your head down. And yet this kind of presentation format is used time and time again within large organizations in the honest belief that it is good communications practice. Worse still, it has featured prominently in many change management projects. Naturally, there is a role for these major presentations and open meetings – especially when visions or detailed change programmes are being launched – but it is dangerous to rely on them as the sole means of communicating with your people.

To be successful, open presentations must be based around a two-way format. They should include specific slots for presentations from different groups of people who are represented in the audience. Both sides must set out to learn something from each other.

The same goes for email and intranets. How many times have you had a long email from the Chief Executive with a cheery request for comments and queries at the bottom? Can you imagine a junior accounts clerk sending the CEO a response? Unlikely.

It also applies to company magazines and newsletters; they tend to be one-way communications too.

The management of change demands two-way communications. In order for any programme to work, people must have confidence in the vision, the programme and the people who are going to deliver it. They want to have the opportunity to test their senior management's knowledge of and belief in the vision. People need to be satisfied that the person who is leading the programme is personally committed before they will accept it. That means having their questions answered in a range of different ways. Open forums are useful in establishing credibility, providing people with the opportunity to observe how the CEO handles comments and queries from others. It's all part of the confidence-building process.

Of course, you cannot make all communications two-way. There are bound to be occasions when a round-robin email on some aspect of the change management programme is the best way of putting the message across to a wide audience. But my point is that change management is very much dependent on two-way communications and they must feature prominently in any programme. For much of this book I have been referring to how difficult change is for many people, how much they need reassurance, motivation, rewards, guidance and encouragement. All these things demand two-way communications. How can you reassure someone just by talking at them? The only way you can do it is to talk *with* them.

Bear in mind too that people have information coming at them all day long, through many different channels. They get copied in on countless emails, many of which are irrelevant to them; they may have Internet news-links which clog up their inbox; there are internal memos; in-house magazines and other publications; not to mention the pile of trade magazines sitting on their desks.

It all amounts to information overload. Pure noise. So how do people sort the wheat from the chaff, especially in the middle of a programme of change?

The simple answer is that they can't, unless you help them. This places huge importance on the change leader's skills as a communicator and the ability of the implementation team to design and deliver high-quality mechanisms for proper two-way communications. They must take the time to develop a format for team meetings which have mechanisms for effective two-way communications built into them. Careful thought also has to be given to how you make it easy and less intimidating for people to offer feedback on email messages relevant to the change management programme.

Important though it is, let's put communications into the context of the whole programme. Two-way communications clearly have a role to play in determining the way in which the programme is implemented. People's ideas and input are often very helpful in shaping the details of the process. But the vision must remain constant; communications can be used to sell the idea and persuade people about the need for change, but the vision itself must be firm.

One final point about communications is that people make judgements on the accuracy and authenticity of what they are told according to what they see happening around them, especially where this involves senior management. It's important that the people doing the communicating live up to their own messages. In other words, they must practise what they preach.

KEY FACT

Successful change management thrives on two-way communications.

24   The power of accountability

'Life is pleasant. Death is peaceful. It's the transition that's troublesome.'
Isaac Asimov

Accountability breeds commitment. The more that senior executives who 'own' the programme of change can demonstrate that they see themselves as personally accountable for its success, the more people will be committed to it.

When BMW's Jürgen Lubos announced a major change programme at the company's Oxford plant, which produces the new Mini, he made it perfectly clear to the whole workforce that he would hold himself responsible if it failed. And, as anyone who has had anything to do with the British car industry will testify, that was a bold undertaking indeed, especially given that the programme was based around bringing a wide range of people into the decision-making process and the introduction of team-working.

Happily, Lubos's change programme was an outstanding success. Just nine months after the start of the programme, absenteeism and costs per car had fallen dramatically and output had increased by no less than 40 per cent. Clearly the commitment of the workforce to making the programme work was a major factor in its success, as indeed was Lubos's bravery in making himself fully accountable right from the start.

Accountability unquestionably involves courage. It's obviously easier and safer to share responsibility with others, or simply shove it in their direction when things look as if they might be going wrong. But, as discussed in the last chapter, people are always watching to see what their leaders do as well as what they say. If there is just the slightest hint that they may be backing away from the change programme or delegating responsibility for some tricky part of it, then people's confidence in and commitment to the whole programme will deteriorate.

Of course, most chief executives are used to being above the day-to-day management challenges of their people. Delegation comes naturally to them. But with change management they must pick up the gauntlet. This forces them to make absolutely certain that they are comfortable with the vision that they must articulate and live by, perhaps for many years. They also need to have total confidence in the change management team, their implementation plan, milestones and ability to deliver what they promise. Only then can they feel confident enough to take personal responsibility for the programme.

Everyone involved in a change programme has some responsibility for its success, none more so than the person who has the job of keeping the vision alive. Accountability is crucial to the success of the programme.

KEY FACT

People will lose confidence in the leader and the vision at the first sign of buck-passing.

25 Presenting the case for change

'Things do not change; we change.'
Henry Thoreau

Here comes a shock: change is a bad idea. I realize you have been going through this entire book thinking that we all need to be more focused on change, but you're wrong. The problem is that people don't like the word 'change', because it suggests leaving behind something with which you are familiar and happy and making a leap into the unknown. Rather than incorporating the term 'change' into your programme, give it a positive title, perhaps using words such as 'target' or 'challenger'. The second phase of BMW's change programme at its Oxford plant, for example, was called 'Working in Groups' (WINGS).

The title and the best way of presenting it will become obvious once you have thought it through and anticipated the feelings of the people who are going to be on the receiving end of the message. They will tell you, if you ask them, what it is they want to happen. People like to feel they are going to be challenged, when they don't necessarily like to think they are going to be changed.

Even if you do listen to them, they may not of course tell you exactly what they are thinking. People's resistance to change and new ideas isn't always articulated clearly. There is often a mass movement of people all complaining about the same things at the same time, following the general trend rather than thinking things through for themselves. This tendency can be seen at its most dramatic with crises like major strikes or other industrial action. The individuals who do feel uneasy about the way things are going may well not voice their apprehensions or disapproval when asked; it will only come to the surface in roundabout ways through increased cynicism or lack of cooperation. Managers may therefore hear a message coming from below them that does not, in fact, reflect the views of everyone, but only the views of those who shout the loudest.

One of the biggest challenges in presenting the vision and the case for change is to do it with such panache that you immediately alleviate some of your people's natural worries. Of course, people will always have concerns – and indeed they may not communicate them very easily – which have to be addressed as the programme progresses. But you can bring a significant number of people on-side right from the start if you put your vision across well.

I mentioned earlier the value of honesty in change management. This is never more potent than when it's applied at the very start of the programme. Tell your people right from the word go that you will own up if elements of the programme are delayed or unforeseen problems occur. This will have a huge impact on people's confidence and commitment to the problem. They need to hear that they will be kept informed of the ups and downs of the programme as it progresses; there is nothing more damaging than the corporate grapevine. But if you have committed yourself to frankness and openness about the status of the programme as it develops, the rumour mill won't turn so fast.

There is no 'one size fits all' way of communicating a change management vision in a company. Like it or not, there will be people from many different backgrounds in your company. There will be some who are tabloid newspaper readers, others who take the *Financial Times* and some who pick up what they need to know from breakfast TV. You cannot expect to communicate with them all successfully in the same way.

You must take time to segment your audience and then develop the best method of communicating with each group. The trick is to explain why you are giving presentations in slightly different styles and formats to ensure that everybody gets the same message. Consistency, of course, is key.

The use of language in communications is also crucial. It is all too easy to be misunderstood in a letter or e-mail, or even in a short phone call. The language used must be thought through carefully to ensure that it doesn't contain any ambiguities or double meanings, which is often a problem when you are dealing with an international organization.

People will be looking for chances to read between the lines, particularly if there is any culture of distrust (which may be one of the prime drivers for change in the first place). They will be trying to work out what management is 'really saying' when they talk about new opportunities. There can be no room for misinterpretation in any of the messages.

But, of course, the most effective way of communicating is

through action. The message will really hit home when people start to see the organization changing around them. They will be looking for changes in language and tone in all internal communications; they will be looking for signs of a new approach by senior management and an atmosphere of joint endeavour around the company. If people cannot smell that change is really in the air, then there is little chance of gaining their commitment.

It sounds obvious when put in black and white, but it is amazing how many managers will pay lip-service to change programmes and fail to understand the full extent of their personal involvement. They put all their effort into selling the vision, and then behave as if it applies to everyone else except themselves. They create a strong vision, and then they corrupt their message and sabotage the journey before it has even got under way.

It is much easier to see these inconsistencies when you are at the bottom of an organization looking up than when you are at the top looking down. A chief executive will often have his view obscured by clever, politically motivated managers. He will believe what he is told and may have little idea what is going on below the clouds. The workforce, hearing the messages coming from the chief executive's office while at the same time experiencing what is actually happening at ground level, will be able to see very clearly how the vision is being distorted and corrupted along the way.

It's also worth bearing in mind that change management is not just an internal issue. It is bound to affect customers and suppliers too. What do you tell them about the programme and how it's going to benefit them? You should not be shy of briefing them about the vision you are working to internally and about the structure and timing of the programme. They will need to have confidence in it too, but not in the same way as your own people. Communications with external audiences may not be of the same intensity but will still require careful management; all you are trying to do is give them a positive message about what you are doing and why you are doing it and keep them posted on your progress. Shareholders will also be very interested and they will be keen to ensure that the programme is going to deliver what it promises. They will also be anxious that it should provide a good return on investment.

When Luc Vandevelde went public on his massive change management programme for Marks & Spencer, he ran through it in great detail at the company's Annual General Meeting, believing that it was important for the City to understand the true scale of the transformation he had planned. And he was right: it was a turning-point in the company's relationship with the markets and confidence started to return to the stock from that point onwards.

When the market's confidence in a company is low, everyone wants to see change. The first sign is usually the appointment of a new Chief Executive and other senior directors. The next thing everyone wants to hear is what the new team is going to do to transform the company's fortunes. That's why major change programmes go down so well in the City.

There is also a clear relationship between a change programme and the company's brand. If the programme is successful, it should add value to the brand. As a result, many companies use change programmes as an opportunity to enhance their corporate identity, perhaps supporting this with advertising, PR and new literature. But there is a risk attached to this if, for some reason, the programme is not a complete success or if, as in some cases, it is abandoned altogether. The timing for any corporate design or communications activity needs to be handled carefully. Clearly, any investment in this area should ideally coincide with the successful completion of the programme or a key milestone in the final stages, by which time success is more or less guaranteed.

It is also important to keep your internal audiences briefed on any brand communications activity relating to the programme. Show them any new identity design and related advertising in advance and brief them on any corporate PR programme you may have planned to mark the end of the change process.

Of course, the external audiences are important; they will all sit in judgement at the conclusion of the programme and take different views on what they have gained from it. But it's the internal audience that the change management programme needs to pay most attention to and who should therefore be your top priority. Sometimes, of course, the City has to be briefed on a change programme in advance because it may have implications for shareholders. However, whenever possible, tell your own people first.

KEY FACT

Change programmes must be communicated externally as well as internally. But the tone and style of the messages are very different and the internal audience should normally be the top priority.

26 Selling the dream

> *'The reasonable man adapts himself to the world; the
> unreasonable one persists in trying to adapt the world to himself.
> Therefore all progress depends on the unreasonable man.'*
> George Bernard Shaw

Many of us still remember the way in which Rupert Murdoch took a sledgehammer to the print unions in the late 1970s. His ruthlessness and grim determination to bring about change in the newspaper industry and break the stranglehold of the old Fleet Street trade unions on the streets of Wapping.

The miners' strike in 1984 was a similar battle of wills between the government, led by Margaret Thatcher, and the union that had brought down the Conservative administration a decade earlier. And having won the battle, Mrs Thatcher then sealed her victory by privatizing the few profitable parts of the mining industry and closing the rest of it.

There are many who would look back now and say that these titanic struggles were worth it because they delivered a permanent change in the way British business was run. It was a fight we had to have, they might say, in order to modernize our economy and give us a chance of competing in world markets. But at the time people were far more sceptical about the causes and questioned the need for all that strife.

In fact, most people are dubious about change programmes when they are first announced. It's important to anticipate this and be ready to reassure them and answer their questions. This is all part of the selling process to help them see that the change programme is both desirable and achievable.

If your people think the vision is simply a leap too far, you will not be able to take them with you. Equally, if you demonstrate the same attitude as Rupert Murdoch, people may worry about the high price of change. Perhaps, they will think, they could end up as casualties rather than beneficiaries. Overt aggression and determination to bring about change – no matter what and at any price – will distance you from the people you are helping to change. Such an approach will tend to create a climate of fear, one in which people will give the appearance of co-operation but all too often will actually simply be watching their own backs. This can lead to a culture of malicious compliance.

You have to sell the vision and the change programme as desirable, achievable and positive for everyone involved. This means explaining exactly why it's necessary; and how the various milestones in the programme will be reached, and then painting a picture of what life will be like in the land of milk and honey.

Effective change management is driven by clarity, confidence and communications. People do not respond well to aggression and blind ruthlessness: even though sometimes they might work, they invariably carry a cost. Selling the vision in a detailed and positive way will always engage the people you need to go through the change process.

KEY FACT

The vision needs to be sold so effectively that everyone in the company believes they dreamed it up for themselves.

Part Three:
Leading and Managing Change Successfully

27 Making the vision a reality

'For all that moveth doth in change delight.'
Edmund Spenser

One of the great benefits of the milestones approach is that it ensures that everyone involved in the change programme is accountable. This avoids a problem which can arise with long programmes perhaps extending to three years or more; many managers think they will not be around by the end and they therefore can duck responsibility for its success or failure. This tempts leaders to come up with ever more extravagant and unattainable visions and encourages change managers to put together overambitious implementation programmes.

You cannot get away with that if you have regular reviews with milestones. Everyone involved, from the vision-makers to the change managers, can be held to account, which concentrates their minds on establishing practical, achievable goals and programme plans at the start of the process. It also encourages the necessary groundwork by researching and analysing the organization's current culture.

Having decided on the vision, the starting-point for the programme is communicating it to the company. This sounds easy enough, and perhaps that's why so many people stumble at the first hurdle.

Communicating the vision is not a one-person, one-off task. It's something for which the leader and everyone involved in the programme must share responsibility. Furthermore, it's something they are going to have to do time and time again through the duration of the whole programme.

For this reason, it's crucial that everyone at the top of the organization fully understands the vision, can sell it and can answer questions about it. This learning process is key to the success of the whole programme. If the people at the top of the company cannot communicate the vision in a totally consistent and confident way, then the change programme itself cannot succeed. A single moment of public confusion between senior managers will plant the seed of doubt in people's minds about the programme and can damage the leaders' credibility. Remember that the management of change is fragile; like great literature, change programmes are based on the willing suspension of disbelief. There are many dangers to this delicate sense of confidence, not least of which is any sign of weakness, inconsistency or lack of courage on the part of senior management.

Then comes the really tricky part. Having communicated the vision and got everyone at the top of the company to give a consistent message, somebody has to work out exactly how the process of moving towards the delivery of that vision is going to work. And then they have to communicate that too to everyone in the company.

The truth is that the development of the vision can be hugely stimulating and rewarding in its own right. Rather too many leaders and senior management think that that's where their involvement ends. All they have to do is come up with the vision, tell everyone about it, put it on the company intranet, knock up a few posters and newsletters, and Bob's your uncle, the job's done. Worse still, many of them think that once they have 'blessed' the vision, they can simply carry on in the same old way. Wrong. Everything must change from that moment. And every manager must perform his or her job in a way that reflects the values and vision of the change programme going forward.

KEY FACT

Accountability is key to successful change management, and milestones force managers to take responsibility, be transparent and become personally engaged in the process.

28   Articulating the strategy

'Change has a considerable psychological impact on the human mind. To the fearful it is threatening because it means that things may get worse. To the hopeful it is encouraging because things may get better. To the confident it is inspiring because the challenge exists to make things better.'
King Whitney

Anyone who has ever had a flutter on the Grand National will have watched horses, perhaps one they have backed, refuses a fence. You can see the jockey doing everything he can to encourage the horse to go over, but in the end it makes up its own mind and just pulls up, and there is nothing at that point that the jockey, the owner or the luckless punter can do about it.

Change management is rather like a steeplechase. Your job is to help people believe that they can get over all the fences and complete the course. You can encourage them with thoughts about the prize that awaits them at the end of the race. You can try to persuade them that they have the strength and ability to get over the fences and complete the course. You might well have to ride them hard at the fence and then give them a good prod with your heels just to make sure you get them over safely.

The key word here is BELIEF. People must believe that the change programme is rational and achievable within the timetable that has been set for it. Furthermore, they must believe that they can achieve what is being asked of them.

Confidence is everything.

When the privatization and break up of the old British Rail was announced, alongside the creation of Railtrack, few people inside the old BR believed that change was either possible or desirable in the relatively short timescale allowed. Leaving aside the ideological problems that many BR people felt about the abandonment of a national institution, the majority simply had no confidence in their ability to deliver the change. They felt that the gap between where they were at the time of the announcement and the government's vision was too great. As a result, people did not buy into the process that had been established to deliver the vision.

In sharp contrast, look at how BP handled a multi-tiered change programme when it merged with Amoco. Not only did it have a programme supporting the merger itself, it simultaneously ran three other major change management initiatives including a structural reorganization, a new environmental strategy and the refocusing of its human resources function. On the face of it, this looked like a highly ambitious, not to say complex, exercise. But the company worked hard to convince its people that the vision was right and the processes to bring it about were achievable. Through intensive internal communications and consultation, the company secured the confidence of its people. They believed that they could get over all the fences that the company wanted them to jump and that they would win the race.

KEY FACT

Confidence is an essential component of all change management programmes. People must BELIEVE they can play their part in achieving the overall goal.

29 Trusting the new broom

'Change as the winds change, veer in the tide.'
Algernon Swinburne

Many programmes of change come about as a result of a crisis: a collapse in sales, sustained losses or simply an inability to keep pace with a changing market are typical examples. In these circumstances, change is likely to be led by an individual or a group of people new to the organization. And there is usually a real sense of urgency about the need for change.

When Luc Vandevelde took over as chairman and Chief Executive of Marks & Spencer in 2000, he realized that much was expected of him. Change was already underway within the company as it battled to restore its fortunes. He needed to evaluate those changes quickly and then alter and supplement them as necessary.

There was tremendous pressure on him from the board, from the City and, indeed, from Marks & Spencer's own employees to deliver results quickly.

Given his knowledge and experience, it must have been tempting for him to arrive at the company with some ready-made solutions to the group's woes and implement them immediately. But he had the good sense to start by spending a few months going round the company introducing himself, talking to people and listening to what they told him about the current change strategy. Of course, he needed this internal intelligence, but even more importantly, he needed to win people's confidence in him as the new broom. He knew that putting the company back on its feet was going to be a huge team effort involving a restructured board with everyone in the company playing a part. So he spent those first few months doing three things: formulating his change strategy, learning what was wrong with the current one and selling himself to the people.

When Vandevelde came to make his speech to the 2001 AGM, he was able to set out an impressive and detailed vision for change. He spoke about the need for the company to focus on the UK market, to deal only with its own brand, to achieve better segmentation in clothing, to expand its food business, to revamp many of its stores, to reform its supply chain and to bolster the profile of its financial services operation. His vision touched virtually every part of the business and everyone in it. Moreover, the breadth and richness of his vision for change made it clear that it was based on massive internal consultation. Although he was addressing the AGM, it was obvious that his vision was directed as much at employees as it was at shareholders. The key point is that he had won his people's trust and was presenting a credible, achievable vision.

KEY FACT

New brooms are often under pressure to deliver major changes quickly. But you cannot develop a change programme without first understanding your company, its markets and its people. Once you have that knowledge and your people's confidence, you can move ahead fast.

30 Changing attitudes to authority

'Any change, even a change for the better, is always accompanied by drawbacks and discomforts.'
Arnold Bennett

Change management is ideally suited to people with modern ideas on leadership. But it's more challenging for people whose thinking is more traditional.

The old hierarchical order in Western countries has changed dramatically. The days when you respected your boss simply because he had a bigger office and a grander title are now long gone, just as we no longer respect someone simply because they are older or a member of a particular profession. In more and more situations, people are judged by the results they produce and the way they behave. It is a much healthier way to structure a society, but it also brings with it problems and confusions, and the change from the old hierarchical structure to the new meritocracy has been a long and painful journey. It is a transition that still has some way to go in many companies.

In some areas of Western society these changes have caused considerable problems. Schoolteachers have difficulty controlling children who are not willing to do as they are told and who show them no respect. Priests see the number of parishioners dwindling as the general population becomes less content to be told how to live their lives by religious leaders who sometimes seem to be out of touch with ordinary people. Doctors find that their patients no longer treat them with the reverence they would have taken for granted 30, or even 20, years ago; they question diagnoses and treatment they are given and even go looking for unofficial second opinions, whether from alternative practitioners, medical books, newspapers or the Internet.

Everyone now expects to be treated as an individual. They may go to someone in order to benefit from their expertise, but that doesn't mean they will automatically respect them or do as they are told.

So what do people respect in business if not seniority, experience and knowledge? They certainly respond to successful people, those who prove themselves time and time again either within their own company or as entrepreneurs. Sir Richard Branson remains a business icon in the eyes of the under-45 age group. This is no more than you might expect in a meritocracy.

However, there is another group of people commanding almost universal respect these days. They are the innovators: the 'ideas people' who challenge conventional thinking and dare to make a success of doing things differently. Look at the way George Davis the fashion entrepreneur transformed Asda by introducing his low-cost branded clothes into the supermarket. He challenged conventional thinking by saying that people would walk out of Asda with a trolley full of groceries, six pairs of pants and a pullover. And they did.

Then there's Stelios Haji-Ioannou, who started the whole low-cost airline market. His thinking was pretty simple: people wanted a no-frills, short-haul service which would save them a lot of money. They would put up with inconvenient flight times and all sorts of other service compromises if the price was right. The industry and its observers scoffed at the idea and the rest of the story is, as they say, history. With the success of EasyJet, Stelios became a modern-day hero. Now he is set to challenge conventional thinking in the world of cinema and hotels.

As a change manager in your company, you are in a unique position to earn the respect of your people. You have the opportunity to be an innovator, an ideas person. More importantly, like George Davis and Stelios, you can turn these ideas into reality within your own organization.

You need people's respect and trust in order to be a successful change manager. Do not underestimate the potency of creativity as a tool for getting people on your side.

KEY FACT

Seniority and status count for little in today's business world. If you want respect and influence as a manager of change, then you must prove yourself as a creative thinker.

31   Putting wrong changes right

*'If you don't like something, change it. If you can't change it,
change your attitude.'*
Maya Angelou

Preparing your company and your people for change and getting
them used to the idea is clearly a positive measure. But change does
not always work; indeed, sometimes it can be incredibly destructive, especially if the process is not managed properly.

Marconi is a good example of a company that almost destroyed
itself with change. It had a successful history as GEC, which built a
reputation as a strong company capable of profiting well in the
good times and riding out the storms. But Marconi's refocus on
telecommunications at the height of the boom in the 1990s proved
to be a catastrophic mistake. Not only did the board invest in
internal systems and refocus large numbers of its people, it also
embarked on a programme to acquire telecoms companies and
went very public about its new strategy. This was an example of
change management without risk factors being taken into account;
there was no safety-net, no opportunity for the company to hold up
its hands and say 'Look, I am sorry everybody, this just isn't
working out as we planned; we are going to have a rethink.' They
appeared to have gambled everything on a market which was at the
top of its cycle.

The company's global change programmes had barely begun
before things started to go wrong. Management processes and
workflows were not fully evolved; rather than resolving these huge
operational issues, the board became totally focused on debt
management and investor relations. Its failure was inevitable.
Thousands of people lost their livelihoods and millions of shareholders were left high and dry.

The dotcom boom is also littered with examples of reckless
change management. And it wasn't just the Internet entrepreneurs
who plunged in, genuinely believing that the world had changed
forever. Many large companies jumped on the bandwagon;
investing millions setting up online businesses or divisions, intro-

ducing new technology, retraining their people and establishing different processes. Major retailers, supermarkets, holiday operators and insurance firms are just some examples of companies that rushed headlong into the 'Internet era' and are still nursing huge losses. Then there are the large companies and government departments who invested heavily in e-procurement systems in the belief that the Internet would instantly revolutionize their supply-side processes. Well, it might one day, but it's all going to take a lot longer than everyone imagined. Meanwhile, offline procurement continues to be an important function for most large organizations.

The bottom line is that all management of change needs a safety-net. You must find the balance between a positive focus on a specific outcome and a willingness and ability to change course if circumstances demand it. It all goes back to one of the key benefits of the culture of change: if people are constantly ready for change, they will accept that even in the middle of a change management programme some aspects of it may need to be adjusted. The vision always stays the same, but people will understand that the route taken might have to vary in response to changing market conditions or other pressures. Returning to our plane journey example for a moment: you may find you have to take a different flight from the one you were booked on, or change planes somewhere, in order to reach your destination. It's the same when you are sailing and the wind changes: you might have to tack, but that does not alter your overall course.

KEY FACT

The best managers of change are the ones who can admit they have made a mistake and can alter the course of their programme, if only slightly. If you have a culture of change in your organization, people will be flexible and adaptable, not condemnatory, when the programme is adjusted.

32 Facing the financial truth

'You must be the change you wish to see in the world.'
Mahatma Gandhi

There is no escaping the fact that change management can be expensive. That's not surprising if you are seeking to alter the whole focus of your company: think of it as an investment that will generate a huge return if you get it right.

However, many change management programmes fail because they are seen as a cost rather than an investment. There must be a commitment to support the programme right the way through and beyond. Remember that change management should mean permanent change, which almost certainly involves a rethinking of your cost-base in the longer term.

Developing the financial model for the change programme and agreeing sources for long-term funding are important parts of the planning process. Obviously, you can only get a clear picture of the investment needed once you have agreed the vision, the timing and the implementation programme. But the funding line needed for the programme must be agreed in advance and guaranteed.

There is nothing more damaging than having to scale down, compromise or even abandon a change management programme because of a change in budget priorities. It's a bit like not taking the full course of antibiotics: the problem you are treating not only remains, it becomes resistant to the medication. So it is with the management of change: if you start a programme and then stop it, it's hard to get back on track. One way to avoid this is to take funding for change initiatives outside of the annual budget review process, with the money guaranteed for the full term of the programme no matter what. Furthermore, this sends an important signal in itself to your people about your company's commitment to the programme.

Again, it's worth bearing in mind what you are trying to achieve with change management. You are setting out to implement change to your business operation. Having made the decision to embark on the process, you have an obligation to your people and your shareholders to protect its funding and deliver the outcome you promised them.

KEY FACT

Change management needs guaranteed funding for the full term of the project. If you cannot make this guarantee, then you are not serious about the change you want to make. This is an investment, not a cost.

33   Combating resistance to change

'None of us knows what the next change is going to be, what unexpected opportunity is just round the corner, waiting a few months or a few years to change all the tenor of our lives.'
Kathleen Norris

The older we get, the harder we find it to change. You can extend that idea to entire countries and economies. For instance, in Western and Northern Europe, with our long industrial economic histories, empires, and so on, we have grown comfortable with 'our way of doing things', even though it has not always been successful. All new ideas are looked at with a collective arched eyebrow of suspicion and measured sceptically against current business methods and thinking.

But in America, the Far East, and even parts of Eastern Europe that have emerged into the free world after decades of communist rule, new ideas are the lifeblood of the economy. Small wonder that America, for example, has almost singlehandedly driven the global computer industry. Virtually all the major IT breakthroughs – the personal computer, the word processor, the spreadsheet, the Internet, inventions that have changed the world over the last 25 years – came from the United States. Not only that, but many of the great management and business thinkers have also come from across the Atlantic.

The tiger economies of Asia take their lead from the United States; they have been quick to pick up new ideas, new technologies and new ways of doing things, undeterred by thick layers of commercial tradition and deeply embedded processes in their own countries.

In many parts of Europe, however, they find change difficult. People and companies simply cannot keep up with the pace of change from the United States and elsewhere. They seem to want time to evaluate ideas and inventions, to consider them against what they have already before making a commitment to adopt them. And by the time managers get round to making any sort of decision, the next wave of innovation comes sweeping across the Atlantic.

The use of the Internet is a good example. While America surged ahead with e-commerce and Internet usage soared, the European Union debated issues such as consumer rights, sales tax and customs duties. As a result, many parts of Europe still have very low Internet usage rates compared with other regions of the world and commercial opportunities have been lost. This isn't the place to discuss the rights and wrongs of the EU's approach, but merely to point out that Europe is sometimes slow to react to and take advantage of technical innovation.

This natural caution about new ideas and methods varies in intensity. People working in international companies, especially those who travel widely as part of their work, are very often the least conservative and most open to new ideas. Indeed, many of them pride themselves on being in touch with the latest technology, the hot new management thinking, business books and buzz-words.

But for every one of these jet-setters, there are tens of thousands of people who rarely set foot outside their home town during the course of their work. They are the bedrock of many European economies, and a lot of these people are resistant to change. And let's not forget the vast number of people working all over Europe in the public sector, which is steeped in outdated working practices, old technology and attitudes that, in many cases, have progressed little since the Second World War.

It's hardly surprising that change managers sometimes find life difficult. They could be seen as a threat by a large proportion of the working population.

It's important not to underestimate this collective resistance to change. You should also understand that, rather paradoxically, people don't like to *appear* to be against change. They like to project an image of being adaptable and open, keen on innovation. But, in reality, many conceal a steely determination to keep things just the way they are.

So how do you break the back of this aversion to change? The simple answer is that you have to demonstrate to people that they will benefit personally from your programme. But be careful here. What you think is beneficial may not be so to them. Perhaps they are used to working at a certain pace. It could be that there are parts of their jobs that are very easy and undemanding and they like doing them. They may not see it as exciting to be trained to use a new piece of technology or to move to a smarter, modern office. They may not even be motivated by the opportunity to earn more money. Older junior and middle managers, especially in the public sector, often have a value-set that managers of change find hard to penetrate and understand.

You have to get under the skin of the work culture you are dealing with before you put forward the benefits of change. And often it boils down to using the carrot and stick approach: you might also need to light a few platforms to make people realize that the old ways of working are disappearing anyway.

However, many good, positive, hardworking people who appear to be locked into a traditional way of working are surprisingly receptive to change management. I remember watching the scales fall from the eyes of a group of public-sector junior managers who were transferring to our company as part of an outsourcing contract. It was a moment of true enlightenment when they were told that when they joined us they would be seen as an asset rather than a cost. We told them that we would invest in them with the expectation that there would be a return over time as their careers developed. The message hit home, and they responded very positively to the programme of change.

KEY FACT

People will only embrace change when they can clearly understand how they will benefit personally from it. But there is no 'one size fits all' solution. People see things differently.

34   The importance of feelings

'Without change, something sleeps inside us, and seldom
awakens. The sleeper must awaken.'
Frank Herbert

So far in this section, we have outlined the key elements of a change
management programme:

- understanding the true nature of your organization before you
  begin
- developing the vision
- planning the programme
- selling the vision
- working to key milestones.

The remainder of the section deals with the less tangible issues such
as communications, risk management and maintaining the
momentum of the programme.

Communications is the lifeblood of any change management
programme. In the final analysis, it is the single most important
success driver, because if you fail to communicate with your people
properly, you cannot hope to carry them through the change process.

But what do we mean by communications? As mentioned in
Chapter 23 in the context of change management, there are two
types of communications: one-way and two-way. Many senior
managers find it very hard to accept that they must listen as well as
tell. To them, the most important issue in a change management
programme, especially one with a tight timescale, is to tell people
what is happening and to keep them informed. When the Post
Office introduced its ill-fated name-change to Consignia, it spent
millions on communications, much of it directed at its own people
explaining to them why the name change was needed, and what the
new name meant in terms of potential brand value. There was little
or no consultation with front-line employees when the name was
under discussion, and no mechanism for evaluating feedback from
customer-facing people once it was introduced.

This was a classic case of people being told, kept informed, if you like, and a good example of one-way communications being used when two-way communications were what was really needed.

Compare this with the way communications were handled at Marks & Spencer, where change appeared to be much better planned. The company started its change process by stating a simple objective: to regain and then hold on to market share. But it recognized that the question of how it met this objective was not going to be answered in detail simply by the top management team sitting round a table. They went out and talked to the company's greatest asset – its people – and consulted with them in depth. They also kept on going back to them as the change management plan took shape, gathering people's views at every stage. The plan that finally emerged was a real root-and-branch change programme involving a new strategy for working with suppliers, new designers and big changes in store management. Every single cog and wheel in the company was involved in the change process. More importantly, all employees felt as if they had played a part in shaping the company's future and developing the strategy. As a result, everyone in the company was personally committed to making the change process a success. The communications were constant and two-way; the company's management set out to listen as well as tell.

People's attitude towards their company and their role within it is highly complex, more so than most senior managers imagine. Very few people see themselves as simply 'doing a job, earning a crust'. Most have a degree of pride in what they do and have strong feelings about the organization for which they work. If you listen to people talking in the office restaurant, on the phone or at meetings, most of them have ideas for doing things differently, thoughts on how the organization could improve itself. Often these suggestions come across as moans and complaints. But underneath it all, most people really do care about their company.

That's why it is so dangerous simply to tell people about major changes. Never assume that people are indifferent to how their organization is going to change, and certainly don't assume they only see change management from the perspective of how it may affect them personally. Of course that will be high on everyone's agenda, but it will not be the only issue.

Dialogue is the most undervalued form of communication. First, often the best, most practical ideas for making your change programme successful will come from your own people. So if you don't talk to them you will lose that potentially valuable input. Second, if you want people's co-operation, the best way of getting it is to make them feel they have played a part in the development of the change management plan. Third, most people have a complex relationship with the organization for which they work. Their sense of pride is fragile and it requires careful handling, especially when it comes to the management of change.

When General Electric began a global initiative to move the majority of its internal processes online in order to cut expenses and improve productivity, it consulted widely within the company on the details, encouraging people to propose ideas on how maximum savings could be achieved in their own departments through this process re-engineering. As a result, the company saved more money than it expected and the bulk of the programme was completed ahead of schedule.

The truth is that people are a crucial resource for most organizations. If you tell them about your change programme and you don't involve them in the development of the process then you stand to be penalized on two counts. First, you are denying yourself access to your own people's ideas; second, you risk damaging their sense of involvement in the direction of the organization, which is demotivating.

If people are not motivated to make your change programme a success, then it simply cannot work.

KEY FACT

Your people probably have many good ideas for achieving change. But if you don't talk to them properly and listen to what they say, you will never know. The more of their contributions you take on board, the more support you will have for the overall programme.

35 Technology take-up

'We are chameleons, and our partialities and prejudices change places with an easy and blessed facility, and we are soon wonted to the change and happy with it.'
Mark Twain

It's often hard to predict the speed with which technology will become embedded and change a market. It always takes longer than the hype would suggest; for instance, it was years before mobile phones really caught on, and laptop computers took their time too. But if you believed the marketing and PR at the time, you would have thought that all these inventions were going to change the face of business the minute they became available.

Business managers have learned to be circumspect about technology and its benefits. These days they are more likely to make their own judgements than simply accept the views of the market. But in years gone by, panic buying of new technology was the norm because nobody wanted to be left behind. It was more a matter of acquiring the technology than of making any practical use of it. Witness the herd mentality that drove billions of pounds to be wasted on early Internet technology and supporting processes.

Ask anyone in IT sales today and they will tell you the same story about how times have changed. You can only sell technology now if you can demonstrate a return on investment.

So how does this impact on change programmes, given that they frequently involve the adoption of new technology and an accompanying change of processes?

The simple answer is that senior management's more considered, hard-nosed approach to buying new technology can be a real help to change managers. People know that nothing is bought these days just because 'it's new technology and therefore it must be good'. It has to be reliable and deliver proven financial benefits.

Managers have come to understand the need for training, new processes and change management programmes in order to make the best use of technology. Few managers these days would simply adopt new systems and tell their people to get on with it. Any return on investment would be unrealizable if they did.

These days, therefore, technology is no longer seen as a threat as it was when Rupert Murdoch used it to transform Fleet Street in the early 1980s. The Luddite mentality has given way to a more pragmatic, positive attitude. Most people see the arrival of new technology as an opportunity to learn new skills, often highly marketable ones, at their employer's expense.

You only have to go and visit a well-run contact centre to see clear evidence of this change of attitude. I have met middle-aged former miners from South Wales and redundant steel-workers in the North-East who have learned new computer skills and found well-paid, healthy and satisfying jobs in modern contact centres.

The same is true in many local authorities, large companies and government departments. The introduction of technology has given thousands of people a new lease of life, providing them with highly valuable skills and making them more productive. And they know it. Very few could even imagine going back to their old ways of working.

Yes, some people will always be frightened of new technology and worried about their job prospects and handling new processes, and you will meet resistance. But don't underestimate people's willingness to adopt new technology, learn new skills and enhance – rescue in some cases – their careers and long-term employment prospects.

KEY FACT

The vast majority of working people today see technology as a personal opportunity rather than a threat.

36   Changing role-based cultures

'Times change and we change with them.'
Anon.

Role-based cultures, which are most commonly found in the public sector and in large, traditional companies, are hard to change. If people have been indoctrinated over many years to believe that titles and status are earned through loyalty and length of service, it can be extremely difficult to introduce modern ideas of performance measurement and rewards based on merit.

Many organizations have deeply embedded belief systems that have been built up, layer upon layer, over many decades. Despite successive UK governments' attempts to change the public sector, many parts of it still suffer from a powerful undercurrent of traditional workplace values, which they find almost impossible to shift. Time-serving, status and judging people by their grade rather than their ability are all still prevalent. And, of course, the trade unions still have a huge influence in the public sector, which adds to the difficulties of bringing about radical change.

Government after government has tried and largely failed to create a new culture in the public sector and drive up the quality of service it delivers. They have been held up by a lack of investment, resistance to change and an element of cynicism that seems to greet every new initiative. You can't help feeling that the main reason that real reform has never happened is that successive governments have just not grasped the nettle.

Let's take local government as an example. The rewards and benefits system for employees and the basic grading structure has not changed fundamentally in decades. Restrictions on capital expenditure have prevented most local councils from investing in new technology. As a result, old systems, out-of-date processes based on these systems and overmanning are still common. But worst of all, many departments within councils have incompatible technology and databases. This makes it extremely difficult for council departments to communicate with each other and has a direct impact on quality of service. This is one of the reasons why, when you call your Town Hall, you get passed from one person to another and it usually takes what seems like an age to get anything done.

It's no good pointing fingers at the people or institutions that might be to blame for this situation. The big issue is how we can bring about radical change.

Clearly, technology is key. Open systems, integrated data and communications and greater use of web-based services could break down the old ways of working and dramatically improve the quality of many people's lives – employees and citizens alike. It also highlights the need to raise the level of partnership with the private sector, to enable the right expertise and resources to be applied to the problem.

However, there is still considerable resistance to private and public partnerships from political dogmatists and public-sector traditionalists. The notion that the public sector is good and the private sector is bad still prevails. Local government desperately needs new technology, new ideas, flexible benefits and the intro-duction of a performance-related culture in order to drive up productivity and encourage creativity. The private sector can pro-vide this impetus for radical change.

KEY FACT

Motivation is the key to increasing productivity. If you can encourage public-sector workers to see that they have something personally valuable to aim for, then wholesale change is possible.

37 Working with trade unions to bring about change

'I don't recognize you – I've changed a lot.'
Oscar Wilde

Ask any modern trade union official to explain their role and it's likely that the idea of protection will feature in the answer. This has probably always been the case; the unions first came about because of the need to help working people, with a focus on improving pay and conditions. It was a radical movement which was born to bring about badly needed change and to challenge the industrial status quo.

However, these days, the unions are much more focused on protecting what they have achieved, particularly over the last 50 years. They are in the business of protecting jobs and defending working practices and reward systems. On the face of it, in the early twenty-first century, the unions seem to be against change rather than for it. But you would be wrong if you thought that. It's dangerous to stereotype trade unions as difficult, always against change and new ways of working. Many realize that the world has moved on; Europe is in the post-industrial age and the trade unions know that if they are to maintain their relevance to their members and play a role in modern business they have to change too.

Yes, they still have their traditional concerns: jobs, pay and conditions. But many are now also very focused on career development for their members, re-skilling, training and the benefits that people can gain by taking a flexible approach to their work.

At Syntegra, we worked closely and effectively with many trade union leaders to bring about major change. We have moved entire departments from the public sector into the private sector; we have created massive contact centres, retraining employees drawn from all parts of large companies; we have introduced significant new technology which has transformed the way organizations work, changing virtually everybody's job in the process; and we have replaced traditional pay packages with systems of flexible benefits, giving people much more influence over how they are rewarded.

In most of these cases we have negotiated and then worked with trade unions to manage change. Often they have been a positive and creative influence in the process.

KEY FACT

Many trade unions recognize that they can play a positive role in change management initiatives and deliver major benefits for their members. Be sensitive to the union agenda, of course – remember that their first loyalty, as they see it, is to their members – but at the same time don't stereotype them.

38 When things get personal

*'The biggest men and women with the biggest ideas can be shot
down by the smallest men and women with the smallest minds.
Think big anyway.'*
Kent M. Keith

Let's be under no illusion here: there will always be people who
will do almost anything to derail major programmes of change.
And it can get very personal indeed, because the best way of
wrecking a change initiative is to undermine the people who are
trying to bring it about.

I have come across some extraordinary cases of people being
blackmailed, accused of corruption, receiving hate mail and even
death-threats, both at home and at work, simply because they are
leading or involved in radical programmes of change. I have also
encountered instances of libellous pamphlets and newsletters,
always anonymous, being circulated. Some people's determination
to resist change knows no bounds.

This reinforces the need for change managers to build networks
of contacts and relationships outside their own organization. When
the going gets very tough and personal, it really helps to get
informal guidance from experienced people in your field who are
not connected with your business and can give you objective
advice.

The best way of dealing with the aggressors is to factor them into
the risk plan: to be ready for them. The more radical the change
programme, then the tougher the resistance you are likely to meet.
But never go into any programme expecting everyone to just roll
over and go with it. You are bound to come across the whisperers
and the rumour-mongers, and you might well find some people
have the courage to oppose you openly. Have your arguments
ready; be prepared to meet opposition.

The second way of handling the doubters is to isolate and marginalize them. Give them and everyone else the opportunity to see
that they are in a small minority and have little credibility. Offer
them help, more information, any kind of guidance you can, but do

not give them the impression that you are going to change the programme just for them. Your objective must be to get them on board, not to compromise the goal.

Managers who put themselves forward as champions and insti-gators of change must be prepared for this kind of backlash, particularly in large, role-based environments.

Watch out too for the culture of 'malicious compliance': people who appear to be going along with the change programme – who might even give you the impression of being enthusiastic about it – but then do everything they can behind the scenes to sabotage it.

KEY FACT

In radical programmes of change, personal attacks are inevitable. Isolate and marginalize your opponents and then set about winning them over – but don't compromise on your key objectives.

39 Establishing milestones

'The lapse of ages changes all things – time, language, the earth, the bounds of the sea, the stars of the sky and every thing about, around and underneath man, except man himself.'
George Byron

It's important not to underestimate the value of milestones. They not only serve as genuine measures of progress, they are also an opportunity to reinvigorate the change progress, celebrate achievements, resell the vision, reassure people about what the programme is trying to achieve, realign the programme around external events and factors if necessary, and keep everyone focused.

A bit like the vision, milestones must be credible; if they are not, people simply won't take them seriously. To achieve this, milestones have to include very specific, numeric goals. It's no good saying, for example, that your first milestone for your customer-support department is 'To have made progress towards greater customer satisfaction'. The question is: exactly how much and by when? Furthermore, you have to be completely open about how progress is being measured, especially if this involves qualitative research. What was the sample size? What questions were they asked? When was the research carried out? Obviously, this becomes easier if the milestones are based around the number of people moving into new roles, different offices or going through a specific training programme, and so on. There can be no argument or equivocation about those measures.

Milestones clearly have to be mapped out against two criteria. First, what is realistically achievable within the relevant timeframe; and second, the length of the overall programme and its outcome.

Obviously, everyone involved in the change management process is working on the basis of achieving their milestones. But failure to meet a target is not necessarily a bad thing. First, from an internal PR point of view, a failure can bring people together, not to attribute blame but to discuss the issues collectively, learn from what went wrong and then agree ways of putting things right before the next milestone. It's all part of the vital communications process, and gives people a sense of purpose. A setback is also an opportunity to rebrief everybody on the vision and the process for getting there, and to reinforce some key messages about the programme.

However, the management of change is more than just a vision and a few milestones. The milestones must spring from the change plan, the detailed programme that will plot the specific actions involved in the change process, allocating tasks and responsibilities to every member of the change management team. They will need to work to their own timescales and milestones and involve themselves in an almost continuous internal review process.

The change management team is bound to involve people who have full-time jobs within the company. It is essential that they are given time and support to fulfil their roles within the change management team, which may involve them being seconded. If you don't have sufficient resources to manage your change programme, then you must get help (see Chapter 20). There are many excellent consultancy firms which specialize in change management. Whatever you do, don't cut corners on project management: it will result in missed milestones and a loss of confidence in the programme. If you are serious about change, it's going to cost money. Face it or don't do it.

KEY FACT

Milestone failures can work to the programme's advantage: they bring people together, refocus them on the value of a collective project and give you a chance to restate your goals.

40   Starting at the top

'Don't fear change, embrace it.'
Anthony D'Angelo

The Chief Executive of a travel agency group had worked hard at his vision. He had gone through all the hoops and tested it thoroughly. Yes, it was bold. Yes, it was exciting. And yes, it was achievable. Over the next five years he was going to build a leading online travel company, by investing in a contact centre and launching a new brand. The high street operation would continue and work alongside the online business, but he would be creating some great opportunities for experienced people to transfer to the new business. He told his people that he believed his strategy would double the size of the company. His vision was the creation of a 'global virtual-travel enterprise within five years'.

The vision raised certain questions. What was going to happen to the high street operation if the online business really took off? People pointed out that he made no mention of the existing bricks-and-mortar business in his vision. Did this mean it might be sold eventually? The Chief Executive said he remained committed to both businesses but that everyone would benefit from the success of the online enterprise. He had plans to float the business and all his people would be offered shares and options. The clear inference was that his people would be rewarded if they co-operated with the plan.

The Chief Executive made it clear that this was his baby. He was personally going to lead the development of the new business and the change programme that would be needed to bring it about.

He ran a series of events visiting every region where his firm had a presence, briefing employees on his vision and his plans for achieving it. He followed this up by including some of his key points on the company intranet and in-house newsletter.

But then there was a long silence. The CEO was a good internal communicator and frequently emailed employees. The online revolution hardly ever got a mention. Then one day the CEO announced that he had handed responsibility for the project to a senior regional manager.

It was at this point people lost faith in the project. The manager who was suddenly delegated to handle the change management programme failed to inspire people. All his words of encouragement and enthusiasm sounded flat and secondhand (in fact they were, because he used the same language and phrases that his boss had employed when he launched the plan). Worse still, the CEO hardly ever mentioned the online business or reported on its progress. It seemed to the people working for him that he himself had lost confidence in the whole project.

There are some important lessons to be drawn from this example.

Change management does not have to be the brain-child of the CEO. In fact, there are many benefits in the initiative coming from a group of senior managers, which may or may not include the CEO. Creativity is often most powerful if it is seen to come from a team.

The job of the CEO, however, is to 'own' the project for the company as a whole. That does not mean that they have to manage the implementation personally. In fact, it's important the CEO appoints a change management team with an overall leader at the start of the project. Notice in the example of the travel company how the CEO took on personal responsibility for the change project and then handed the job to someone else when other business priorities crowded in on him. This was the kiss of death for the whole programme. However, had he established an implementation team and a manager at the beginning of the programme, things would probably have turned out very differently. He would still have been seen to 'own' the vision, lending the whole project huge credibility even though much of the responsibility for the success of the programme would have been shared with other managers and the implementation team.

In some companies there is actually a strategy team whose main purpose is to come up with a vision and plan for the journey, rather like a cabinet working beneath a prime minister. The prime minister may be the one who is associated most strongly with the government's strategy in the minds of the general electorate; he may be the one who articulates it most often as if the vision is his own; but it is most likely that it has come about as a result of team discussion in the cabinet room or has emanated from some other source such as a 'think-tank'.

In other cases, the leader might have only a limited view of the position he wants to take, and will surround himself with people who are able to develop the thinking so that the vision can be articulated and administrated effectively. Some leaders might be capable of producing the whole package themselves, but they are rarities and no company should rely on them to do the job completely.

The most important point though is that once the vision is established, the leader is perceived to be absolutely behind it.

Has there ever been a vision more articulately or powerfully communicated than Martin Luther King's 'I have a dream' speech? There could be no question in the minds of anyone hearing those words that they were spoken by someone who truly believed in what he was saying and doing. So convincing was he that the only way his opponents could think of stopping him was by assassinating him. Margaret Thatcher is another good example of a leader who, at the height of her powers, was able to make people believe wholeheartedly that the vision she was vocalizing was her own. Her downfall was brought about by her becoming detached from the rest of her party. She took too strong a stance on the vision and its execution and was unable to carry her team along with her. In the end her strengths were interpreted as weaknesses, but not before she had achieved a large part of what she had imagined was possible.

KEY FACT

No fundamental change can take place unless it is led convincingly from the very top of the organization. However, people need to see evidence of an implementation team at the start of the journey.

41 Supporting the leader

'If you never change your mind, why have one?'
Edward de Bono

The minute a company launches a programme of change, its world changes. It's like running a marathon: once the starter's gun has gone off you have to keep going until the end of the race. You cannot run for a bit, pop off and do a bit of shopping and then return to the race later. Well, you can if you like, but you are not going to be among the medal-winners if you do.

So it is with change management. It's a continuous process that pervades every aspect of the company's activities. You can't have days or hours when you catch up on the change management process and then leave it for a few weeks.

It can be an exhausting process. Senior management must be working within the change framework the whole time. Every action they take must be set in the context of the change management programme; it takes real vigilance and teamwork. There must be constant contact between the CEO, senior management and the change management team, not just to review progress but to focus on how fresh challenges, changes in market conditions or external events may affect the change plan.

There is no doubt that change management demands both leaders and managers. And often the managers need to 'manage' the leaders. For example, managers should brief the leaders when there are important messages about the programme that need to be conveyed to or discussed with your people.

In a change programme leaders define the vision and direction of the company and set an example, stating the values and setting out the things that are important to the organization. Managers, on the other hand, manage the operational elements of the programme according to predetermined measures for assessing its success.

It's a team effort. And from the rest of the company's point of view, it's important that the leaders and the managers are seen to be working together in a cohesive way.

Remember that the management of change is a difficult balancing act. People can easily lose confidence in the programme and the people leading it, especially if they were sceptical in the first place. If they get the impression that the CEO or leader is losing interest or has become detached from the change management process or vision, then the whole programme may be jeopardized.

It's also important to realize that people will be watching the CEO the whole time, dissecting his every word and every action for evidence of his commitment. The CEO must always lead by example. It's hard work for CEOs; but that's what they're paid for, and it's what real leadership is all about.

KEY FACT

Change management is a constant process. Once you fire the gun on your programme, you must stay in the race to stand a chance of winning.

42 Uncovering the current culture

'If we don't change direction soon, we'll end up where we are going.'
Anon.

I know the CEO of a leading technology company who refuses to have an office of his own. In fact, he doesn't even have a desk. He spends his time working in different offices all over his company, never staying more than a couple of days in the same place.

He has certainly become proficient at 'hot-desking' and mobile working, but that's not why he does it. He runs his life this way because he says it's the only way he can find out what's really going on inside his company and his market. He engages with people the whole time, listens to them talking among themselves and on the phone and joins in their meetings whenever he can. He works on sales pitches, helps collect debts, gets involved in detailed HR (human resources) issues and has even played a part in looking after the company's fleet of vehicles. Nobody knows more about his company and the way his people work and feel about their work than he does.

If anyone understands the true culture of the company, this remarkable man does. But how many senior managers operate like this? Probably very few. It's very easy to become wrapped up in dealing with colleagues at your own level and the next layer down, focusing only on the big issues that preoccupy senior management. But this naturally limits your exposure to people at the grassroots of the organization.

The truth is that all change programmes depend on the people who are planning them having a crystal-clear picture of the true company culture. This includes more than just a view about 'how things are done'. It encompasses the history of the company; its place in the market; people's attitudes to their work; the benefits and promotion system; the structure of the organization; relationships between departments and individuals and between managers and their people; and the level of understanding about the company among employees, including its goals, structure, size, protocols and processes.

It's dangerous for senior management to assume that they know their own company inside out. Just because they have worked for the organization for quite some time – many years perhaps – does not mean that they really understand the complexities of their own company's culture.

You must start any change management initiative by conducting a detailed analysis of the cultural characteristics of your company, organization or institution. That means setting up a team of people – perhaps some external consultants – to go round your company and research all the components of the culture. Only when you have a true picture can you really understand the starting-point for your change programme. Indeed, only then can you begin to develop a vision which your people will see as exciting, credible and achievable.

KEY FACT

As a senior manager, you may think you know your company culture; you probably don't. Invest in proper research to discover the true culture, because this is the essential starting-point for a successful change programme.

Part Four:
Profiting from your Success

43   Creating a 'joined-up' organization

'To change and to change for the better are two different things.'
German proverb

Most companies have come to understand the benefits of having a 'joined-up' organization whereby all departments and people are working towards a common goal. It is underpinned by a culture of reward based on merit, openness, accountability and communications. In a joined-up organization people are able to see their role in the context of the whole organization and learn to value the part that everyone plays in its success.

It's easy enough for small and medium-sized companies to create such a culture, but it's much harder for big organizations, which may have grown used to their old role-based, hierarchical structures and traditions. But the truth is that the 'joined-up' culture is a pretty essential platform for effective change management. It's hard to run a company-wide change programme if people are wedded to a system which, by its very nature, is resistant to change.

Under these circumstances, the first thing that has to change is the role-based structure. That merits a particular kind of change programme, which will almost certainly involve significant reorganization and senior personnel changes, particularly at head of department level. There is little or no point in attempting any more market-orientated change programmes until the company has gone through this essential hoop.

Being joined-up is also about communicating effectively across the cultural and functional boundaries within companies and countries. There are subcultures in any organization; people in finance, in sales and in human resources all have a different outlook and a different way of interacting with each other. There is often rivalry between different departments, of course. But much of this can be mitigated by the creation of a joined-up organization.

The one big advantage of going through the process of creating a joined-up organization just prior to the launch of a major internally focused change programme is that it gives you an opportunity to isolate and deal with potential problems.

For example, you can take out your stovepipes – those structures or groups of people deep within an organization which are purely based around their own internal functions. These are especially prevalent in old-style finance, production, personnel and IT departments. They may see their function as more important than the company itself; they can be inflexible, process-orientated and unhelpful to others. Not surprisingly, they will also be resistant to change.

You can set new standards and protocols for communications and educate people on the need for interdepartmental dialogue. You can also get them used to the idea of limiting the time for internal meetings. In one company I know, there is a strict rule that no meeting should last longer than half an hour, and none of the meeting rooms has chairs. People are encouraged to use email, but they are not allowed to copy an email to more than four people. The theory is that this stops people needlessly clogging up people's in-boxes.

The rooting out of stovepipes and the creation of sensible standards for communications all help to build the right cultural base for a full change management programme. If this culture has been newly created, a change management programme is the ideal application for putting it into practice and ironing out any difficulties.

KEY FACT

You need a 'joined-up' culture for full-scale change management projects to work. If you are still operating a role-based culture, then change that first before tackling anything more ambitious.

44 Recognition and reward systems

'Change begets change. Nothing propagates so fast.'
Charles Dickens

One of the key characteristics of an organization that has success-fully adopted the culture of change is that its people become valued as individuals. They are seen as an asset, rather than a cost.

This means taking a radically different approach to managing people's relationship with the organization. First, if you are going to treat people as individuals, would you pay them all the same amount or give them identical benefit packages? For instance, it doesn't make sense to force a single man in his late twenties to make the same level of pension contributions as a married woman in her fifties. Their financial and personal circumstances are very different. And so too probably are their tastes. Why should we have to take a company car, five weeks holiday and private health insurance? What if we don't want a car (preferring to pay less tax perhaps) and would rather have more holiday?

As mentioned in the last chapter, if one of the stated goals of your change programme is for people to become more flexible, then you have to be flexible in return. Equally, if you want people to feel valued as individuals, then give them choices about how they work and how they are rewarded. To my mind, this is an essential ele-ment in the creation of a flexible, focused workforce who will be receptive to change, and, indeed, become part of a continuous teaming culture.

But there is another important strand to this: recognition. People like their contributions, achievements and good ideas to be recog-nized and rewarded. Not only does this make a person realize that she is valued, it also makes everybody else in the organization feel positive. They like to see that individual effort and successes are noticed and that it's not just salesmen and senior management who are recognized.

Of course, it's important that any reward system encapsulates the company culture and vision, but it must also reinforce the vision for the change programme. At Syntegra, for instance, we operated a peer-group recognition system whereby anyone in the organization could nominate anyone else for awards. The nominator and nominee met with a director, were photographed and generally celebrated, often involving other colleagues; they also received a certificate as well as a financial reward. This system worked very well, largely because the recognition is initiated by employees themselves and senior management becomes involved only at the moment of celebration.

KEY FACT

If you want to create a culture of continuous change in your organization then you must treat people as individuals. You should also be reflecting this in the way you recognize and reward people.

45 Recruiting for change

'Progress is a nice word. But change is its motivator. And change has its enemies.'
John F. Kennedy

Organizational change normally involves the recruitment of new people. This might mean new faces at the top of the company, new heads of department and the introduction of new teams in parts of the business that have been underperforming or are the main focus of any programme of change.

One of the big dilemmas for many companies embarking on a change programme is whether they should recruit the new people first and then start the change programme, or the other way round. Unfortunately, there is no simple answer, because every situation is different, though it's hard to conceive how a company could undergo a major transformation and then bring in a new CEO halfway through. Certainly, if the change is radical, then new people should be in post to lead it.

However, whatever the case, there is no question that the recruitment process and the change programme must be very closely integrated. New people, especially senior managers, must be entirely tuned in to the change process and reflect all the qualities of the overall vision.

Therefore the timing of the recruitment of key people and the process you use to bring in new appointees to the company needs special attention.

On the question of timing, most companies seem to work on the principle that a drip-feed approach to recruitment as the change management programme progresses is the best strategy. They are alert to the danger of bringing in too many new people at once, upsetting the equilibrium within the company as it goes through a carefully planned transformation. Equally, they appreciate that introducing the right people at the right time can enhance and even accelerate the change process. Timing is crucial; you must strive to ensure a critical mass of people in your organization actively support the change programme.

Milestones present great opportunities for new people to join the organization. If you are using the achievement of milestones properly they will be occasions for celebration: a chance to look back at what you have achieved with some satisfaction and look at the challenges ahead with confidence. So they are ideal occasions for introducing new people, who quickly become immersed in the vision to help current employees move on to the next milestone. This process of gradual recruitment can be repeated throughout the programme, so that by the time you reach the key objectives you have your new team entirely in post.

However, recruitment in the context of change management requires a very different approach from the normal HR process. For instance, who should be managing the brief and the selection? Should it be your current HR managers, who may be too closely associated with the past culture of the company? Are they the right people to be choosing recruits who are being brought in to help the company go through a fundamental change? It may be that you need to put your own HR department through a change process before you involve them in the recruitment project. Otherwise, there is a danger that they will be too tied to past standards. In most change programmes it makes sense to increase the level of involvement of your senior management in the recruitment process because they will be closest to the vision and the overall goal.

Clearly, you will be looking to recruit people with the key skills you need to bring about the change vision. But you will also be looking for people who are highly adaptive, strong internal communicators and who come from organizations whose cultures you admire or are seeking to emulate. In many ways, when you are undergoing a change programme, those latter qualities are as important as the former.

It certainly helps to bring new recruits into the change programme quickly. This places great importance on the development of an induction process that reflects the change management vision and the remaining milestones that need to be passed before the company can achieve it. It would obviously be counterproductive to use the old induction process and then introduce the new recruits to the change management vision and programme, but an amazing number of organizations do just that.

KEY FACT

Your new recruits are agents for change, but take care how you select them and who you use to handle that process. Involve your senior management in the recruitment programme as much as possible.

46 Changing people's perceptions of themselves

'There is something in the pang of change, more than the heart can bear.'
Euripedes

If you are in sales or marketing, you are a contributor; but if you are in finance or HR, you are a cost. Completely unfair, of course. But sadly, that's how a lot of people see themselves and others in a large organization. Worse still, that's clearly a view shared by quite a few senior managers, because when they need to cut jobs to save money, they always seem to start with the business support functions: IT, finance, HR, and so on. The problem is exacerbated by the fact that some senior managers wrongly assume that only low-quality people are attracted to work in support departments. If people see themselves simply as a cost item, in the firing-line to be cut when times get tough, they are almost bound to be demotivated, uncommitted to the company and far less effective than they should be.

On the other side of the coin, I have known some pretty average sales executives who feel that they are invulnerable, always safe in their jobs provided they hit their targets. This is because they feel that their contribution to the company is visible and measurable.

One of the great opportunities of change programmes is to make everybody in the organization recognize that they can become assets rather than costs. It's important to change people's perceptions of themselves so that they all regard themselves as equally valuable contributors to the company. That does not necessarily mean putting the sales and marketing team in their place; it's more a question of elevating the feeling of self-worth among people who may have seen themselves as part of 'central costs'.

This may involve a number of separate initiatives.

First, people in business support departments often feel detached from the front-line: indeed, that's one of the origins of their sense of vulnerability and lack of visibility. Therefore, one of the most pressing tasks is to connect them more closely to so-called contributing departments, such as sales. Internal communications and interdepartmental projects, ideas forums and partnering will all help to achieve this.

Second, it's important to establish a rewards system that recognizes the support departments. The achievements and efforts of their people should be recognized and celebrated throughout the company. This means rewarding the accounts clerk who manages to reduce her debtors list and improve the company's cashflow, or the recruitment manager who fills ten key posts a month ahead of schedule. If these are celebrated around the company then not only will the people concerned and their colleagues start to feel that they are important to the company but the recognition of their efforts will also mean the more front-line departments put their own role in perspective. That's why it's important too for senior management to be personally involved in the recognition and reward process, particularly when it includes people from business support departments.

Change management can only succeed if you can build a culture in which everyone feels that they are valuable and that they recognize the contributions of others. It's also important for people to see they are part of the team, willing to help others at any time in order to achieve a common goal.

KEY FACT

If people fully understand their value to the company, to each other and to their team as a whole, they will work more effectively to increase it.

47   Training for change

'To keep our faces toward change, and behave like free spirits in the presence of fate, is strength undefeatable.'
Helen Keller

Not that long ago, training was one of the first budgets to be slashed the minute a company started to hit hard times. But things have changed; most large organizations now realize that through training they can add considerable value to one of their greatest assets, namely their people.

Indeed, training is often written into people's conditions of employment. Some trade unions, for example, have succeeded in securing free training and education for their members in a whole range of fields, many of them with little or no relevance to the work that they do. In other words, in many cases training is seen as a perk.

When an organization undergoes a programme of change, training is one of the most important tools in the box. It should be utilized to help people use new processes, learn IT and develop other skills directed towards the delivery of the vision. People need to understand that every training course they attend, whether a one-day session or a week-long residential programme, makes a measurable contribution to the change programme by improving their skills or knowledge in a specific way.

Therefore, the whole perception of training as a benefit or as something that delivers learning that 'might be useful some day' must change.

Every training course must be evaluated against its contribution to the development of the skills needed to enable people to move from one milestone to another. Only by doing this can you successfully integrate training into the change management process, and elevate its status from a perk to a necessity and increase the skill capacity of the organization at the same time.

Good training gives people confidence, delivers focused learning and makes them feel valued. Above all else it gives them an incentive to change and develop. That, of course, is an essential requirement for any change management programme.

KEY FACT

Effective change management thrives on good training. Make it relevant and focused around the goals of the programme. Training should be used to motivate people as well as to develop key skills.

48 Changing attitude: the party test

'Weep not that the world changes – did it keep a stable, changeless state 'twere cause indeed to weep.'
William Bryant

When you meet someone at a party, it never takes long before the conversation gets round to the subject of work (especially if it involves two men for some reason). One of you is bound to ask: 'So, what do you do then?'

I am always fascinated by the different ways in which people respond to this question. In an instant you can gain an impression of whether they are happy and motivated at work or bored and frustrated. Here are three typical responses:

'I'm a finance manager.'

'I work in finance.'

'I work for British Airways.'

Each one of these answers tells a story. The first suggests that the person is quite status-conscious and indicates that he is relatively senior with people reporting in to him. He is making a statement about himself. It tells me that it is highly likely he is from a company with a traditional hierarchical culture. Perhaps his response also suggests that he may value more highly his status than the company he works for.

The second answer might imply that the person is unexcited by his work. He does not bother to mention whether he is senior or junior (you might assume the latter, but it may not be the case). Nor does he mention the company he works for. It could be that he doesn't like the company much either. Perhaps he just sees himself as a part of the central costs of the company and thinks that his contribution is simply not noticed by anyone.

The third response is particularly interesting. He is obviously proud of his company, because he mentions that first. It's clearly a positive statement, meant to convey that he thinks he is lucky to be working for an organization like BA. To him, the fact that he works at BA is more important than his job title or specific role. He may go on to describe his job in more detail, but the most impressive thing he feels he has to say is that he works for BA. To him, it says something about him.

One of the benefits of effective change management is that it engenders in people a sense of pride about the company they work for; they are glad to be part of a great team. Yes, you want people to feel that their role is important, that they are valued and are contributors to the company's overall success. But above all, you are trying to create a culture whereby people feel connected to a vibrant, dynamic organization that responds quickly to market conditions.

The culture of corporate or organizational pride should be one of the goals of a change programme. When it comes to the party test, the successful outcome is that the person being asked about what he does for a living puts his company first.

KEY FACT

One of the outcomes of successful change programmes is that people take renewed pride in their company. This creates a platform for further change, provided people can see how it will benefit the organization as a whole.

49   Measures of success

'Examine what you believe to be impossible, and then change your beliefs.'
Dr Wayne Dyer

Completing a change programme should be an emotional moment, a bit like reaching the finishing-line having run a marathon. But, unfortunately, very often change management isn't like that; for many companies there isn't a point when everyone feels they have 'got there' and won their medal. More often than not the programme is extended or moves on to another, perhaps overlapping with the first. Having created a continuous culture of change, the company and its people will feel they must be constantly developing in line with the needs of the market.

So how do you know if you have succeeded in delivering the vision? I think there must come a point when you can measure the effectiveness of the programme and, you hope, declare it a success. You owe it to the people you have taken on the journey to tell them when you arrive at important staging posts. They deserve to know whether their hard work and commitment has paid off. And I think it should be a cause for real celebration! This in itself is an important internal PR message and will help you to gather people's support for the next change programme when it comes.

In many ways measurement is relatively easy. If you have been managing your programme properly, you will have been running a system of milestones throughout the process. Given that these are based on time and the achievement of specific goals, each one would have given you an opportunity to look back at how far the organization has come and the distance you still have to travel. As you get towards the last few milestones, you should be able to see the finishing-line. This is often the point at which companies consider introducing a new phase to their change programme, perhaps in response to external events or market fluctuations. Having created the culture of change, it's in their interests to make immediate use of it. Fine. But I firmly believe that people should be allowed to see each programme completed, even though there may be an overlap with the next. Let them get to the final milestone and enjoy the experience but at the same time accept that continuous change must become part of their working lives.

Milestones are only one measure, of course. Bear in mind that they were established at the very start of the programme, so they may not be the most precise barometer of success. As much as anything else, milestones are there to focus people's energy and enthusiasm.

So, to be confident that your programme has succeeded you need other measures.

Within the change management team and the programme plan it is important to establish key success factors at the start of the project. These might include:

- reductions in the number of people within specific teams
- cost reductions in key areas
- transfers of people from one department to another
- number of new recruits introduced to the company
- reduction in employee turnover
- degree to which processes have changed and are working effectively
- increase in customer numbers and satisfaction
- reduction in the time to market for your goods or services
- growth of revenue and profits.

All these are easy to measure against targets set for specific dates.

However, most change management programmes involve more than just moving employees around, cutting or adding people and re-engineering processes. Most are focused on more abstract issues such as:

- customer attitude and behaviour
- employee attitude and productivity
- culture change with the purpose of creating a different environment in which to do business.

There is no escaping it: these must be measured before you can take a view on the success of your programme.

This involves ensuring that you carry out pre-programme research and then repeat the same process at key points during the programme. Your research must be a combination of both quantitative and qualitative for it to have any real meaning. Ideally, it should involve a number of interviews with people, assessing their attitude and behaviours before the programme starts. Then the whole exercise has to be repeated at set intervals.

This should be supplemented by focus-group research among all the target audiences.

Even though you may have in-house expertise in this field, it's best to get professional advice. The last thing you want is people challenging your research findings by picking holes in your methodology. You don't have to hire one of the big firms and spend a fortune; talk to the Market Research Society if you would like the names of some reputable firms. But do get the job done properly.

So, in the final analysis, there are three ways of measuring the success of your change management programme:

- the achievement of milestones on time
- the achievement of specific numerical targets for implementing new processes, moving people, cutting costs, increasing productivity and revenue, and improving customer service
- the achievement of targets (which can also be numerical) for a change in attitude and behaviour of your internal and external target audiences.

It's more than likely that you will not complete your programme with a 100 per cent success rate in all these fields. But you and your people will know whether you have succeeded in delivering the vision that inspired the programme and burned like a lighthouse all the way through it.

Whatever the measurements tell you, don't forget to celebrate your achievements.

KEY FACT

Objective evidence is important when you are assessing the effectiveness of your programme. Whatever method you use for measuring your success, make sure that it is understandable, credible and consistent.

50 Maintaining a permanent evolution

'Change is inevitable, except from vending machines.'
Steven Wright

Right at the start of this book I talked about the real objective of change management as being the creation of a culture of learning and continuous change within your organization. Companies constantly underestimate the speed at which their markets are changing; and the reality is that unless they are in a constant state of readiness to adapt they will miss market opportunities with increasingly significant consequences.

This is also true in the public sector, where people's expectations of service have risen sharply over the last ten years as technology has enabled the private sector to provide an ever-increasing standard of service. People now look to the public sector to keep up, but often it doesn't.

And, nice as it would be to have that pool filled with the magic 'change' fluid, people simply cannot shake off old ways of working and thinking and become change-orientated overnight.

The truth is that it is bound to take more than one change management programme to achieve this goal. Indeed, it could take as many as three, or even more. This may sound like a daunting prospect, but it needn't be. One programme can lead seamlessly into another; visions can be extended and expanded until you reach your ultimate goal. The main problem is that people have a limited capacity for change. Imagine you were someone who was quite happy jogging along in a role-based culture, looking forward to your next promotion in a year or two and planning for retirement in fifteen years or so on an index-linked pension. You come into work as usual one Monday and you are told that within two years your entire working life is going to be turned upside down. You are going to change job, move building, learn new skills, deal with many more people, have a completely new range of responsibilities and will have your entire benefits package changed. Can you imagine the reaction? It would be like being told that your wife is leaving you after twenty years of a contented married life to set up home with an old schoolfriend called Mildred!

People who have little or no experience of major change will only be able to take it in bite-sized chunks, certainly initially. That's why it's so important to get the vision right; when they see the challenge ahead of them, people must believe that they are capable of meeting it. Not only that, they must want to do it; they have to be able to see the benefit of making the effort.

In this context, that first change management programme is fraught with danger. On the one hand, maintaining the momentum is key; you have to keep presenting the vision and the reasons for change throughout the process. On the other, people often get fed up with hearing the same old message over and over again. I was once involved in a change programme when people said that they had heard enough. They knew the message, understood it in every detail, and simply did not want to hear it again. So we refocused our attention away from messages and concentrated more on the process elements of the change programme.

Within months, people were questioning the whole purpose of the programme, asking senior management about the strategy and objectives. And, having called for the drum-beating to end, they kept wondering why it had stopped, and were almost in a state of confusion. It proved to me, once and for all, that it is essential to keep plugging the vision. Never shut down the lighthouse: always have it lit so that everyone can see where they should be going.

However, there is no doubt that people do get better at change. Once you have gone through the first programme, they understand what's expected of them. Even more importantly, they will have started to experience the benefits and will have seen that, far from necessarily being an evil thing, change can be beneficial. The next step, of course, is to move on to the next change objective.

Timing is important. If you want to derive maximum benefit from the success of the first programme, you should follow it up almost immediately with the next phase of change. You must make the most of the mood of optimism and sense of achievement at the end of the first programme, because it will soon be forgotten as people get on with their day-to-day working lives. Move in quickly with your second programme. In fact, the best plan is to make the two programmes overlap; get people started on the second before the first one has finished. This is particularly effective if, as is most likely to be the case, the two programmes are closely related. For instance, when you originally designed your change programme, you may have decided that the big vision was too ambitious: that you would be putting up a challenge which people would feel they could not meet. In these circumstances it would make sense to create a two-phased programme, each with its own vision. Clearly, you can only focus people on the vision for the first programme before you move on to the second. However, connecting the visions is important.

No matter how you choose to run your programme and what vision you use to drive it, there are some important subliminal, secondary messages that must be fed in along the way. One of them is simple: your market is changing all the time. And here's another: you must learn to change constantly to keep up with your customers' needs. OK, these messages need professional treatment if they are to be communicated effectively. But people must get used to the idea that continuous change and learning is not only necessary but essential. They must understand, too, that it is not a stop-and-start exercise – change a bit, have a rest; change another bit; have another rest – it is a state of mind and a way of working.

When the chips are down, that is what change management is all about: changing forever the way people think about their contribution in the workplace.

This is a good time to be putting this message across. So many of the pillars of inertia and predictability in the working world are being torn down: final salary pension schemes are disappearing fast; early retirement is being discouraged; short-term contracts of employment are the norm; the tax system (with taper relief for capital gains tax, for example) now favours people being rewarded through stock options and share schemes; at the same time public-sector employers want wholesale changes to working practices and to reduce the cost of service delivery. The list goes on. And on the other side of the fence, customers are becoming increasingly demanding and fickle. We all are; we all want better service and better value from every organization we deal with. These days, nobody is ever satisfied. Whether this is a good thing or not is hardly worth worrying about. It's simply a fact of modern life that we must all learn to accept, because this constant demand for more directly affects the way all of us have to work. We must either accept the culture of continuous change in our work or fail.

I have been working in the field of managing change for many years and have experienced some remarkable results along the way. It still excites me.

KEY FACT

Change management never finishes. Your first programme should immediately be followed by another, until you have created a culture of continuous change and learning in your organization. Quite simply, your survival depends on it.